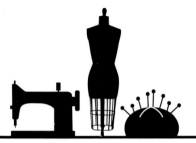

HOW TO SPEAK
FLUENT SEWING

First published in the United States in 2015 by Stash Books, an imprint of
C&T Publishing, Inc., PO Box 1456, Lafayette, CA 94549

© Copyright RotoVision SA 2015
RotoVision SA
114 Western Road
Hove
BN3 1DD
www.rotovision.com

ISBN: 978-1-61745-073-0

Publisher: Mark Searle
Editorial Director: Isheeta Mustafi
Editor: Angela Koo
Commissioning Editor: Jacqueline Ford
Assistant Editor: Tamsin Richardson
Page Layout: Richard Peters
Illustrations: Sarah Lawrence and Rob Brandt
Cover Design: Kristy Zacharias

Printed in China

10 9 8 7 6 5 4 3 2 1

HOW TO SPEAK FLUENT SEWING

The indispensable illustrated guide to sewing and fabric terminology

CHRISTINE HAYNES

stashBOOKS®

an imprint of C&T Publishing

CONTENTS

3: MACHINE TERMS

4: STITCH TERMS

5: FABRIC TERMS

CONTENTS

6: PATTERN & GARMENT TERMS

7: TECHNIQUES & PROCESSES

HOW TO USE THIS BOOK

My favorite kinds of sewing books are resource books. I love researching terms, looking at the illustrations, and learning the difference between tools and weave structures. If you find yourself asking questions like, "What is the difference between a plain weave, a twill weave, and a satin weave?," then this is the book for you! I hope to demystify all those terms, tools, and techniques so you are armed with the knowledge necessary to get the job done.

This book is organized into a series of chapters, and from there, the items are broken down into subgroups. If you're not sure which category a term belongs in, never fear—the index at the back will help you find what you're looking for.

First you will learn about tools in Chapter 1, discovering the difference between cutting tools, marking tools, and closures, to name a few subgroups. After tools, Chapter 2 is all about needles. Get to know about the different kinds of sewing-machine needles and hand-sewing needles, as well as the anatomy of a needle, so you can tell your shank from your shaft!

In Chapter 3, you discover the sewing machine, which is your key tool in sewing. Familiarize yourself with the parts of the machine, different types of machines, and fill in any gaps that you may have encountered in your machine manual. Chapter 4 is all about the many stitches you will utilize when sewing, whether by hand or by machine. You will also see the many stitches it takes to complete a garment, such as understitching, topstitching, and edgestitching.

Chapter 5 is all about fabric, where I will teach you about the many different styles of weave structure and fabric construction, as well as providing lots of lessons on prints, fabric finishes, and fabric treatments. In Chapter 6 you will learn all about pattern and garment terminology, and, to be honest, this is my favorite chapter. Wait until you see the cute illustrations of peplums, skirts, and Peter Pan collars. But don't worry, it's not just full of cute drawings—you will also learn all about pattern-drafting tools and terms, pattern markings, and construction elements, such as gathering, pleats, and pockets.

In the last chapter, I break down the techniques and processes in sewing. Here you will learn the difference between underlining, lining, and interlining, as well as embellishment processes, like huck weaving, tatting, and more.

I truly love how jam-packed this book is with terms and definitions, from the most basic to the much more advanced. I hope you learn something new, and discover a technique, tool, or process to inspire your next project!

Christie Haynes

TOOLS P10

NEEDLE TERMS P50

MACHINE TERMS P62

STITCH TERMS P74

FABRIC TERMS P92

PATTERN & GARMENT TERMS P126

TECHNIQUES & PROCESSES P164

CHAPTER 1
TOOLS

DRESSMAKING SHEARS

WHAT THEY ARE: Scissors with a bent handle, found in a range of sizes from 7 to 14 in (18 to 35.5 cm). In order to keep the blades sharp, they should only be used to cut fabric, thread, and unwired ribbon.

WHAT THEY DO: The bent handle keeps the lower blade flat on the cutting surface, while the sharp blades glide through your fabric.

WHY USE THEM: Cutting with scissors that do not have a bent handle will elevate your cutting above your table, making your cuts less clean and precise. Sharp dressmaker shears will ensure the most accurate cutting, which will in turn make the construction process more exact as well. Precise cutting is the best foundation for a successful project.

TRIMMING SHEARS

WHAT THEY ARE: Small scissors with two finger holes and a pair of blades down the center. Typically they are 5 in (12.5 cm) or shorter.

WHAT THEY DO: Trim thread, seam allowances, notches, and other small applications, when a full-sized pair of scissors are too large to be accurate.

WHY USE THEM: They provide more control when making fine cuts in tight areas, ensuring nothing is cut unintentionally.

EMBROIDERY SCISSORS

WHAT THEY ARE: Small scissors with symmetrical finger holes and a pair of short blades centered down the handle.

WHAT THEY DO: They are used to clip the threads in small and tight areas of embroidery, or other forms of finely detailed needlework.

WHY USE THEM: Clipping in small areas is best done with smaller scissors. There is less chance of error or cutting something accidentally, and the small points offer much more precision than bulky full-sized dressmaker shears.

PINKING SHEARS

WHAT THEY ARE: Pinking shears are scissors with pointy metal triangles along the cutting surface.

WHAT THEY DO: These will cut fabric or paper just like regular scissors, but will leave behind a series of triangles instead of a clean cut.

WHY USE THEM: Some people use pinking shears for their decorative effect, but they can also be used to finish seam allowances on the inside of projects. The angles of the cut keep fabric edges from fraying. Always test on a scrap before using on your project.

CUTTING

ROTARY CUTTER

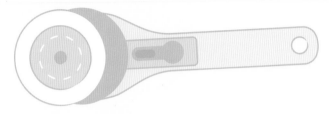

WHAT IT IS: A handheld cutter with a plastic or metal handle and a round razor blade on the opposite end.

WHAT IT DOES: The round blade cuts through layers of fabric. A rotary cutter is best used on a self-healing cutting mat, and with a thick quilting ruler to protect the hand.

WHY USE IT: Mainly used for cutting quilt pieces and blocks, this is a quick and efficient way to make precise, straight cuts.

 SEE ALSO: Quilting, page 88

CUTTING MAT

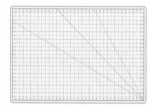

WHAT IT IS: A self-healing plastic mat with measuring marks to use when cutting with a rotary cutter.

WHAT IT DOES: Place the cutting mat on your table and place the item you wish to cut on top. Use the rotary cutter to cut the fabric on top of the mat.

WHY USE IT: The mat protects your table and helps to maintain the sharpness of your cutting blades. The markings on the mat are also very helpful when trimming fabric to a specific size for quilt pieces or when garment cutting.

 SEE ALSO: Quilting, page 88

TAILOR'S CHALK

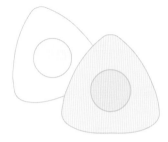

WHAT IT IS: A wedge of chalk that is available in a variety of colors and is safe for use on fabric.

WHAT IT DOES: The chalk surface makes broad stroke marks on fabric that can then be used as guides during sewing.

WHY USE IT: Best used on the wrong side of the fabric or in areas that will not show—it is not usually water soluble—this chalk is ideal for making marking guides for fit and construction.

CHALK PENCIL

WHAT IT IS: A chalk-filled pencil that can be sharpened like a regular pencil. These come in a variety of colors—typically white, yellow, red, and blue.

WHAT IT DOES: It is used to make marks on your fabric for placement, notches, buttonholes, and so on.

WHY USE IT: Being able to mark your fabric provides greater accuracy in your sewing. Chalk pencils come in both water-soluble and regular varieties, so be sure to test your pencil on a scrap before using it on the right side of any project.

 SEE ALSO: Seams, page 168

WATER-SOLUBLE MARKER

WHAT IT IS: A marker that most often has a marking end and an erasing end, though some do not provide the water eraser.

WHAT IT DOES: These leave temporary marks on your fabric to use as guides for sewing.

WHY USE IT: Making marks like this is the best way to ensure precision sewing for elements like darts, buttonholes, and pivots. The marks can be removed by leaving fabric to soak, or in the washing process, leaving your fabric free of any signs of the marker after use. As always, test on a scrap first.

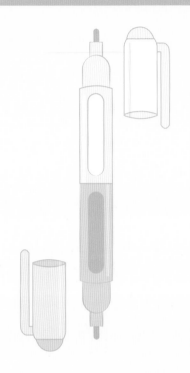

AIR-ERASABLE MARKER

WHAT IT IS: A pen-like marking tool, typically with a marker at one end to draw on the fabric, and an eraser at the opposite end for removing the marks.

WHAT IT DOES: Used for creating reference marks on fabric for darts, pleats, or any other critical spots during construction.

WHY USE IT: Marks will evaporate with time, but can also be removed with the provided eraser or water, making this the perfect tool for marking the right side of your fabric, or spots that will be seen after construction. Always test first!

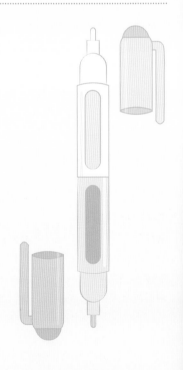

SKIRT MARKER

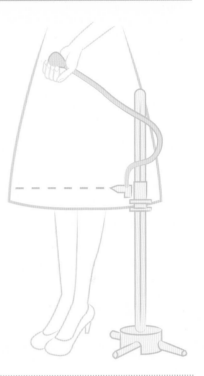

WHAT IT IS: A standing tool with measurements along the vertical pole and an adjustable slider with a chalk insert.

WHAT IT DOES: The variable guide can be raised or lowered to allow the user to accurately mark the hem of their own skirt with the chalk insert, as the marks are made with a chalk power that is blown on by a handheld device. A pin version can be used to mark hems when the wearer has assistance.

WHY USE IT: If you are trying to accurately mark a hem by yourself, the chalk version allows you to be precise when no help is on hand.

HERA MARKER

WHAT IT IS: A small, plastic handheld tool that is used for temporary mark making.

WHAT IT DOES: This marking tool does not in fact make any mark at all; instead it creases fabric to create a line that you can follow.

WHY USE IT: Ideal for use on extra delicate fabrics that need to be kept perfectly clean throughout the entire construction process.

TAPE MEASURE

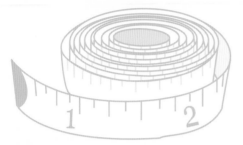

WHAT IT IS: A long and flexible measuring tool, usually 60 in (150 cm) long, with imperial measurements on one side and metric on the reverse.

WHAT IT DOES: A tape measure's flexible nature allows it to be used in areas that are curved, such as around the body when taking accurate measurements for garment construction.

WHY USE IT: When making clothing, precise body measurements are always step one, so that you know what size to cut and sew. Using a flexible tape measure is the best way to get those measurements.

CLEAR RULER

WHAT IT IS: A see-through plastic ruler with measurements for a multitude of measuring needs.

WHAT IT DOES: It assists in accurate marking and measuring in nearly every sewing project.

WHY USE IT: The ability to see the fabric or pattern beneath the ruler is critical for placing pattern pieces on grain, marking darts, hemming, and thousands of other uses. This is one of the most frequently used tools in sewing.

 SEE ALSO: Grain, page 95

EXPANDABLE SEWING GAUGE

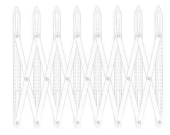

WHAT IT IS: A metal measuring tool that opens and expands in an accordion-like fashion.

WHAT IT DOES: The riveted intersections pivot and the entire tool gradually expands to the required spacing, with each individual section opening by the exact same amount.

WHY USE IT: If you need to mark multiple, repetitive spots of equal distance, such as pleats, or buttonholes down the front of a dress or shirt, then this is a very handy tool.

SEAM GAUGE

WHAT IT IS: A small metal ruler with a plastic slide down the center, usually 6 in (15 cm) long, with imperial measurements on one side, and metric on the other.

WHAT IT DOES: The metal slide can be moved to any measurement along the gauge, setting the distance from the top to the slide. This can be used for making repetitive measurements, or smaller detail measuring when a regular ruler proves too big for accurate marking.

WHY USE IT: Perfect for ensuring distances between buttons are equal, for marking pivot marks on corners and collars, and any other small area needing precision marking.

THREAD

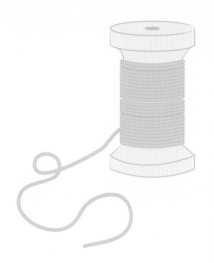

WHAT IT IS: A finely milled fiber available in a wide range of textiles, used for sewing by hand or machine.

WHAT IT DOES: Used in nearly every sewing project, thread holds seams together, is used for topstitching, sewing on buttons, and dozens of additional purposes.

WHY USE IT: As the main item that holds everything together, it is hard to complete any sewing project without thread.

CONE THREAD

WHAT IT IS: A cone-shaped spool holding about 3,000 yards (meters) of thread. Typically only available in 100 percent cotton or polyester.

WHAT IT DOES: Just like regular-sized spools of thread, this holds your seams together.

WHY USE IT: These larger spools are used on industrial and serger/overlock machines, which use up a lot of thread. In addition, the spool pins on these machines cannot accommodate a smaller spool, just as a home machine's spool pin cannot take a cone spool.

 SEE ALSO: Serger/Overlocker, page 73

BUTTONHOLE THREAD

WHAT IT IS: A heavyweight thread commonly made of three-ply silk, with greater durability than construction thread.

WHAT IT DOES: It provides a strong and smooth finish when hand sewing buttonholes, tailoring, or working on other areas that require strong, fine finishing.

WHY USE IT: This thread will create a luxurious and strong bond in detail areas that will get a lot of wear and visual attention. The finish will be both beautiful and durable.

NEEDLE THREADER

WHAT IT IS: A tool that consists of a small handle, with a very thin loop of wire at the end.

WHAT IT DOES: The loop of wire assists with getting thread through the eye of any needle. Thread is looped through the wire, which is, in turn, inserted into the eye of the needle, threading it at the same time.

WHY USE IT: If your hand is not terribly steady, or if you have trouble stabilizing your thread, this tool makes it quick and easy to get the thread through the tiny eye of a needle.

HAND SEWING

NEEDLE

WHAT IT IS: A thin metal needle with an eye at one end and a point at the other. These come in a wide range of thicknesses and point styles.

WHAT IT DOES: Used when sewing by hand, the thread feeds into the open eye at one end, while the point pierces the fabric and pulls the thread through the fabric.

WHY USE IT: A multitude of situations call for hand sewing, such as attaching buttons, hemming, closing up openings, or sewing on trims. Needle types vary according to the fabric being used, so consider this when choosing your needle.

BEESWAX

WHAT IT IS: Pure beeswax or a composite that comes in a block or cake form.

WHAT IT DOES: When hand stitching, strengthen your thread by running it over the beeswax then through a clean cloth or your fingers to remove any residue.

WHY USE IT: Waxing the thread will give tremendous strength and ensure that threads remain intact longer on your fabric projects. It is also ideal for use on areas of strain, such as buttonholes. Test prior to use to ensure the wax will not stain your fabrics.

THIMBLE

WHAT IT IS: A small cap made of metal, plastic, or silicone—available in a range of sizes—that fits over the finger.

WHAT IT DOES: The thimble protects the tip of the finger it is placed on when sewing by hand.

WHY USE IT: When repeatedly pushing a hand-sewing needle into fabric, the tips of your fingers will grow sore. They can also potentially be punctured by the point of the needle. This tool will shield your finger from injury.

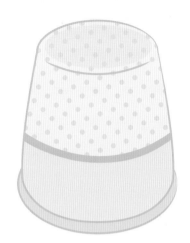

PINCUSHION

WHAT IT IS: A dedicated place for your pins and needles.

WHAT IT DOES: If it is a soft fabric-covered pincushion, pins and needles are stuck into the cushion to keep them orderly. Some pincushions are magnetic, in which case metal pins and needles stick to the face of the cushion.

WHY USE IT: Keeping your pins in one place and nearby is critical during the cutting and sewing process. In addition, as pins and needles are sharp, having a specific spot to place them when they are not in use ensures safety in your home and studio.

GLASS-HEAD PINS

WHAT THEY ARE: Straight pins with one sharp pointed end, a fine metal shaft, and a small glass ball on the opposite end.

WHAT THEY DO: These all-purpose pins hold things together during the entire cutting, sewing, and pressing process.

WHY USE THEM: These are the best pins to use when a project requires you to iron on pinned fabric, as the glass heads will not melt under the heat of the iron when pressed upon, unlike plastic-headed pins.

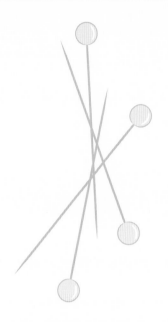

BALL-POINT PINS

WHAT THEY ARE: Used for knit and jersey fabrics, these pins have a slightly rounded tip at the point.

WHAT THEY DO: These pins hold fabric pieces together in preparation for sewing, and help to secure your pattern to the fabric while cutting.

WHY USE THEM: The slightly rounded point will prevent the threads of knit and jersey fabrics from being torn when the pins are pushed through. The point glides between the threads instead of piercing and breaking them.

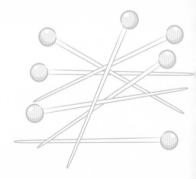

QUILTING PINS

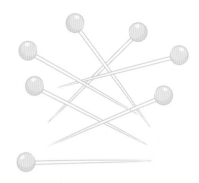

WHAT THEY ARE: Straight pins with large, colored plastic balls on the ends opposite the point.

WHAT THEY DO: These pins hold fabrics together when sewing quilting blocks or adding a binding around the perimeter of a quilt.

WHY USE THEM: The brightly colored balls at the pin ends are designed so that they are easily seen among the many colors and fabrics used in quilt making.

 SEE ALSO: Quilting, page 88

SILK PINS

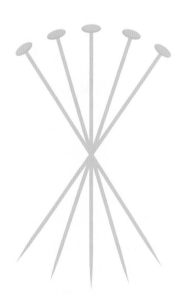

WHAT THEY ARE: Very thin metal pins with a metal, glass, or plastic tip at one end, and a fine, sharp point at the other.

WHAT THEY DO: These delicate pins are used to hold together layers of silk during the cutting or sewing process.

WHY USE THEM: Silk is a delicate fabric that is hard to repair when punctured with a needle too large for its fine weave. Silk pins are extremely fine and are designed to glide through the threads of the silk without leaving a large hole behind.

SAFETY PINS

WHAT THEY ARE: Shaped thin metal closures with a sharp point at one end, a covered clasp at the opposite end, and a spring hinge in between.

WHAT THEY DO: The pointed end unhooks from the clasp and pierces the fabric, then is closed again inside the protective clasp.

WHY USE THEM: Safety pins are used for temporarily holding two layers in place, such as when basting quilt layers together, or pinning in places where the point of a straight pin could prove hazardous.

SNAPS

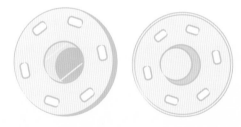

WHAT THEY ARE: Closures with "male" and "female" ends that lock together to form a strong connection.

WHAT THEY DO: One side is sewn or hammered to one piece of fabric, while the other side is attached to a second piece. The two of them are then snapped together to create a closure.

WHY USE THEM: Snaps can be used inside garments to provide hidden closures; alternatively, decorative snaps can be used on the outside in place of buttons. Snaps are also ideal for those who may struggle with buttons, for example, the young or elderly.

FLAT BUTTONS

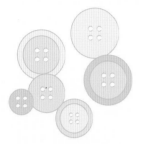

WHAT THEY ARE: Buttons that are flat on both the top and bottom, with two or more holes through the face for sewing to fabric.

WHAT THEY DO: When used with a buttonhole, they close up an opening where two or more pieces of fabric come together.

WHY USE THEM: Unlike a shank button, a flat button has no distance between the bottom of the button and the fabric underneath, so it is best used on lightweight and medium-weight projects. If using on a heavyweight fabric or on a jacket, consider making a thread shank under the button to give it enough lift to span the thickness of the buttonhole.

SHANK BUTTONS

WHAT THEY ARE: Buttons with a decorative top and a metal or plastic loop on the underside.

WHAT THEY DO: A shank button acts like any other button closure, but the lift given by the shank provides extra distance between the fabric to which it is sewn and the underside of the button.

WHY USE THEM: If the fabric used for a project is especially heavy, such as on a jacket, the shank provides sufficient space between the underside of the button and the fabric it is sewn to; this accommodates the extra thickness when the button is done up.

REGULAR ZIPPER

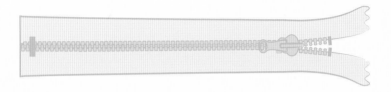

WHAT IT IS: A zipper with zipper teeth on its right side, and zipper tape only on its wrong side.

WHAT IT DOES: The main tool used for creating an openable closure in garments, bags, purses, luggage, and other objects.

WHY USE IT: Many projects call for zippers as the main way to open an object or garment. Unlike an invisible zipper, the regular zipper is fully exposed, or can be hidden under a flap of fabric.

INVISIBLE ZIPPER

WHAT IT IS: A zipper that has the zipper tape on the right side and the teeth hidden on the wrong side. These come in a wide range of colors and lengths.

WHAT IT DOES: When sewn into a seam, it creates a clean closure as the stitching is sewn right up to the teeth on the wrong side, leaving the right side free of topstitching for an invisible opening.

WHY USE IT: Unlike a regular zipper that has a lot of topstitching, with an invisible zipper all the stitching is hidden, making it perfect for the side or center back seam of a dress, skirt, or pants.

METAL ZIPPER

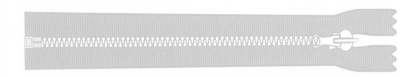

WHAT IT IS: A regular zipper, but with a pull, stop, and teeth made from metal as opposed to nylon or plastic.

WHAT IT DOES: Used for opening and closing garments and accessories, a metal zipper functions just like a regular zipper.

WHY USE IT: For an area with an exposed zipper, a metal zipper offers a nice decorative touch. It is also the strongest type of zipper, making it perfect for areas like a zipper fly on pants, or on luggage and handbags.

SEPARATING ZIPPER

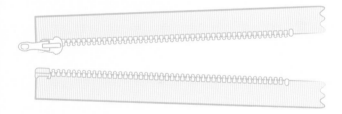

WHAT IT IS: A zipper closure that has a pull at the top and two separate stoppers at the bottom, one on each side of the zipper tape.

WHAT IT DOES: The end of a separating zipper is designed to open completely at the bottom, allowing both sides of the zipper to come apart and fully separate.

WHY USE IT: If you require an item to come apart entirely at a seam and buttons are not a practical choice, this is an ideal closure. It is perfect for projects like jackets and some bags.

CLOSURES

HOOK AND EYE

WHAT IT IS: A small metal two-piece closure, usually in black, silver, or gold.

WHAT IT DOES: The hook side is a J-shaped piece of wire, and the eye side is a wire circle that the hook loops onto in order to close an opening.

WHY USE IT: Perfect for closing up small gaps, such as on waistbands, at the top of zippers on dresses or tops, or similar small openings that need a little bit of closure with minimal strain.

WAISTBAND HOOK AND EYE

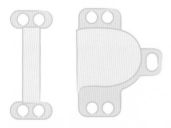

WHAT IT IS: A two-part metal clasp. One side of the closure is a small flat bar, while the other consists of two flat pieces, a small distance apart.

WHAT IT DOES: On the side with two flat pieces, the upper flat piece fits over the bar, interlocking the two pieces together. It is most commonly used at the top of a zipper where two layers of fabric overlap.

WHY USE IT: A waistband hook and eye is typically found in areas where the thickness of a traditional wire hook and eye is too bulky. The flat design of this style keeps the connected layers of fabric nice and flat, giving a smooth outline to the waists of skirts and pants.

HOOK-AND-LOOP FASTENER

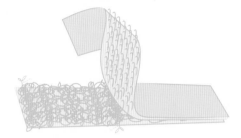

WHAT IT IS: A closure made of nylon or polyester that has "hooks" on one surface and "loops" on the opposite. Available in sticky-back or sew-in varieties, in a range of shapes or in a strip.

WHAT IT DOES: The "hook" side locks into the "loop" side, creating a closure.

WHY USE IT: Ideal for projects that require easy entry and closure, such as wallets, shoes, and children's clothing.

ELASTIC

WHAT IT IS: A rubbery and stretchy trim found in a wide range of styles, widths, and colors.

WHAT IT DOES: Used in waistbands, sleeve hems, and other spots in garment construction, it allows fabric to stretch around the body.

WHY USE IT: If you are designing something without a zipper or button closures but you want the garment to have some shaping, elastic is a good choice. It can define a waist, while still allowing sufficient stretch to get the garment on and off the body.

SLEEVE BOARD

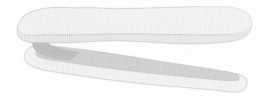

WHAT IT IS: A two-sided mini ironing board that is typically covered in cotton muslin.

WHAT IT DOES: It provides single-sided pressing for tubes of fabric too thin to fit onto a regular-sized ironing board.

WHY USE IT: A sleeve board is perfect for pressing sleeves and other small items that can be slipped onto the end, allowing you to press the top layer and the underside separately.

PRESSING HAM/TAILOR'S HAM

WHAT IT IS: An oval-shaped, firmly stuffed cushion that is covered with cotton fabric on one side and wool fabric on the other.

WHAT IT DOES: This is used for pressing curved seams in a garment.

WHY USE IT: Once fabric has been folded into a dart or shaped into a shoulder and sleeve cap, it becomes a three-dimensional object that can no longer be pressed flat. The ham takes the place of the body part that will later fill the space in the finished garment, fitting into curved seams to act as a mold to press against.

SEAM ROLL

WHAT IT IS: A tube-shaped, firmly stuffed cushion that is usually covered in wool on one side and cotton on the other.

WHAT IT DOES: Similar to a pressing ham, this fills the space left in sewn shapes, such as sleeves, when you are pressing the top layer but not the underside.

WHY USE IT: If there is a seam under the fabric you are pressing, the thickness of the layers might leave an unwanted impression on the surface. A seam roll helps to provide a fill between the layers so that only the top fabric is pressed during ironing.

PRESSING MITT

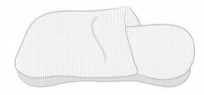

WHAT IT IS: A padded mitten-like object that is worn on the hand when pressing.

WHAT IT DOES: The heat-treated padding covers and protects the hands during the pressing process.

WHY USE IT: A pressing mitt allows you to use your fingers very close to the iron, which is helpful when pressing small details and hard-to-reach areas.

POINT PRESSER

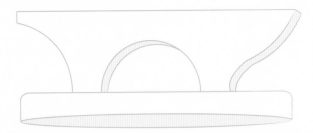

WHAT IT IS: A pressing tool made of solid wood.

WHAT IT DOES: Set the point presser on your ironing board, slip the item over the end of the presser, and then use your iron to press into small areas and tight corners.

WHY USE IT: It lends a helping hand when the item you are sewing has hard-to-reach areas or enclosed corners, such as on lapels, collars, pockets, and cuffs.

TAILOR'S CLAPPER

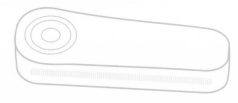

WHAT IT IS: A tailor's clapper is a handheld wooden tool that assists in the pressing process during construction and tailoring.

WHAT IT DOES: After steaming your project, the clapper helps to flatten and crease the item without the risk of burning or marring the fabric with the iron.

WHY USE IT: This tool is used to reduce bulk on heavy seams and seam intersections, or to press a crease in pants. It can also lend a hand in pressing seams open and on other areas where you want to minimize the amount of time that the iron is in contact with the fabric.

NEEDLE BOARD

WHAT IT IS: A wooden board that is covered with closely spaced, blunt, thin, short metal wires.

WHAT IT DOES: It is used when pressing fabrics with pile. Lay your fabric with the nap or pile face down on the board. Set your iron to high steam and hover the iron over the fabric while pressing the steam button. Do not allow the iron to touch the fabric; simply steam the fabric from just above it.

WHY USE IT: The pins on the needle board keep the pile of fabrics such as velvet from getting flattened and crushed during the pressing process.

PRESSING CLOTH

WHAT IT IS: A scrap piece of fabric that is used as a protective barrier in the pressing process.

WHAT IT DOES: Pressing cloths can be used to protect the iron, ironing board, or the fabric itself.

WHY USE IT: Use a pressing cloth beneath your project when pressing with interfacing to protect the ironing board, or use one on top of a delicate fabric to keep the iron from creating a shine on the seams of your project.

SEAM RIPPER

WHAT IT IS: A small handled tool with a sharpened U-shaped bevel and sharp pointer on the end.

WHAT IT DOES: The sharp pointer glides under the thread of a sewn stitch, leading the thread to the U-shaped bevel, which cuts the thread at that point.

WHY USE IT: If you need to remove basting stitches, or take a thread out because of a sewing error, this tool will remove your stitch without damaging the surrounding fabric.

POINT TURNER

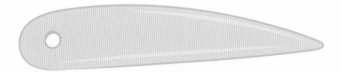

WHAT IT IS: A handheld tool made of plastic or wood with one rounded end and one pointed end.

WHAT IT DOES: The pointed end is used to poke out corners or any angle. The rounded end can help push out fabric on curved seams.

WHY USE IT: There are many occasions on which you need to push out the fabric at a seam and this is best done with a smooth object to avoid breaking the threads of the fabric or the sewn stitches.

BODKIN

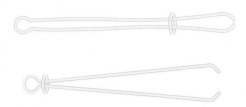

WHAT IT IS: A small metal tool that looks much like a pair of tweezers, with a small circular ring that allows it to open and close.

WHAT IT DOES: The locking ring slides down the tweezers and opens the tool. Simply clamp elastic or drawstring to the tool to pull through casings or other small folded areas.

WHY USE IT: A bodkin is small and slim so it will fit into any size casing. This tool isn't sharp, so if it opens up while in use it is easy to remove and start again, unlike the commonly used safety pin.

TUBE TURNER

WHAT IT IS: Available in a range of diameters, this is a hollow metal tube with a small plastic ring close to one opening, a thin wire with a plastic handle at one end, and a small curl made of the wire at the other.

WHAT IT DOES: The metal tube is fed into a tube of fabric when the wrong side is facing out. The wire is threaded up through the bottom of the tube and is secured to the end of the fabric at the top. When the wire is pulled through the tube, the fabric follows and the action turns the fabric right side out.

WHY USE IT: Especially handy for tubes of 1 in (2.5 cm) and smaller, this tool is a fast way to make handles, spaghetti straps for dresses, belts, and any other tube that requires turning.

STILETTO/AWL

WHAT IT IS: A long metal or wooden stick with a point at one end and a handle at the other.

WHAT IT DOES: It provides a helping hand for feeding fabric into a sewing machine when a project requires you to get close to the moving needle.

WHY USE IT: When there are parts of your project that would be better sewn with your fingers very close to the needle (such as keeping gathers in line when feeding into the machine), this tool is a safer option. A strong pointed awl can also be used to pierce holes in leather and vinyl.

HOOP

WHAT IT IS: Two interlocking circles made of plastic or wood, with a small hand-tightened screw that increases the bond between the two.

WHAT IT DOES: Used in decorative needlework, fabric is placed between the two circles, which are then tightened to create a firm, taut fabric base suitable for beading or embroidery.

WHY USE IT: When creating decorative stitches or delicate beadwork it can be very difficult to sew consistent stitches on loose fabric. By making your fabric taut within the hoop it becomes easier to puncture with your needle.

HEM GUIDE

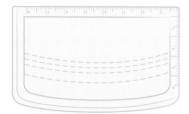

WHAT IT IS: A flat piece of metal with measurement markings to be used as a guide when folding and pressing fabric at the hem.

WHAT IT DOES: This handy tool allows you to fold the hem of a garment to a specific measurement without pinning; you can simply press directly onto the fabric with the guide underneath.

WHY USE IT: Many like this as a shortcut to measuring with a seam gauge and pinning. Since the guide is a bit wide for the hems of pants and sleeves, this is most often used on skirts and dresses.

SEAM SEALANT

WHAT IT IS: A clear and water-resistant gel-like glue that is used on the raw edges of fabric.

WHAT IT DOES: The glue dries clear, sealing the edges of fabric and ribbons to prevent the threads from fraying and unraveling over time.

WHY USE IT: Perfect for use on ribbon ends, on vintage garments with raw edges that cannot be finished without damaging, or on items where a stitch-free finish is desired. It is always best to test on a scrap of the fabric or in a discreet location before using.

DRESS FORM

WHAT IT IS: A soft form in the shape of a male, female, or child-sized body.

WHAT IT DOES: The dress form is used when fitting garments for your own body, if the form is a mirror image of your own shape. Dress forms are also used when draping fabric onto the body in order to design sewing patterns.

WHY USE IT: It is nearly impossible to fit garments in progress entirely on your own body and having a form close to your own shape can prove helpful when trying to envision, design, or shape a garment to your taste and size.

PATTERN WEIGHTS

WHAT THEY ARE: Small weighted objects that are used during the cutting process.

WHAT THEY DO: Used in lieu of pins, pattern weights hold down a pattern piece that has been positioned on top of fabric to be cut out.

WHY USE THEM: If you are using a rotary cutter and do not wish to move fabric around during cutting, weights are a quick way to hold down a pattern. They are also useful for cutting fabrics that are easily punctured with pins, such as silks.

TRACING PAPER

WHAT IT IS: A thin, translucent paper that leaves the layers underneath it visible.

WHAT IT DOES: Tracing paper is used to transfer marks from another sheet of paper. The tracing paper is placed on top, and the marks are made on the tracing paper.

WHY USE IT: To preserve a sewing pattern—whether to make fit changes or because it is irreplaceable—copy the lines from the original to the tracing paper so that the initial pattern can be kept intact.

TRACING WHEEL

WHAT IT IS: A handheld tool with a small spoked metal wheel at one end.

WHAT IT DOES: After securing tracing paper on top of a pattern to be traced, use the metal wheel to make small holes in the tracing paper to then later trace over with a pen or pencil. It can also be used with carbon paper to transfer lines.

WHY USE IT: This is the most effective way to transfer accurate markings from one layer to another.

FUSIBLE INTERFACING

WHAT IT IS: Available in varieties from lightweight to heavyweight, this material is plain on one side and has dots of glue on the other.

WHAT IT DOES: When the interfacing is placed glue side down on the wrong side of the fabric, the heat of an iron will melt the glue and permanently adhere the interfacing to the fabric.

WHY USE IT: Interfacing is commonly found inside collars, on button plackets, on facings, and in accessories such as handbags, giving the pattern pieces additional body and stiffness. Depending on the placement, use the appropriate weight and type of interfacing as instructed by the project.

SEW-IN INTERFACING

WHAT IT IS: A material that is sewn into the inside layers during the construction of a project.
WHAT IT DOES: Adding an extra layer of fabric provides additional stiffness and body to a garment or accessory.

WHY USE IT: Often used in place of fusible interfacing on projects that call for fabrics too delicate or heavy for the fusion of the glue, such as fine silk or wool suiting. Much like fusible interfacing, this added layer supplies additional weight to areas such as collars, lapels, and cuffs.

FUSIBLE WEBBING TAPE

WHAT IT IS: A double-sided webbing available in a variety of widths, sold by the spool.

WHAT IT DOES: Similar to double-sided tape, fusible web adheres two fabrics together when activated by the heat of an iron.

WHY USE IT: Using webbing tape, you can hem garments or home décor items without sewing by simply folding the fabric and fusing the two sides together.

BONDING WEBBING

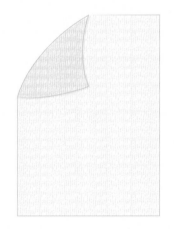

WHAT IT IS: A double-sided fusible webbing that is found on bolts of varying widths.

WHAT IT DOES: The webbing is pressed and fused to one side of the fabric, then fused again on the other side of the webbing. Sometimes this is all done on one fabric; sometimes it involves the fusing of two fabrics.

WHY USE IT: Bonding webbing that is sold by the length is commonly used in appliqué when adhering one fabric to another prior to sewing.

 SEE ALSO: Appliqué, page 175

DOUBLE-SIDED TAPE

WHAT IT IS: A roll of tape with paper adhered to one side and a sticky back side. It is available in a variety of widths.

WHAT IT DOES: Double-sided tape holds together two layers of fabric in situations where pinning is difficult or impossible.

WHY USE IT: This tape is perfect for holding a zipper in place on fabric while sewing, or holding the layers of a flat-felled seam together. Note that it is usually water soluble and can ripple the seam if not washed out.

 SEE ALSO: Flat-felled seam, page 169

WATER-SOLUBLE FABRIC

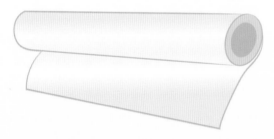

WHAT IT IS: A plastic-like film that dissolves when washed.

WHAT IT DOES: This material provides support when embroidering or creating lace cutouts in fabric. The stabilizer provides stability to the part being worked, and washes away from any surrounding fabric.

WHY USE IT: Trying to do intricate cut work without a stabilizer can prove difficult, so firming up the fabric in advance can help create a perfect result, with nothing left behind.

HAIR CANVAS

WHAT IT IS: An interfacing that is available in both sew-in and fusible varieties, and is typically used in tailored items.

WHAT IT DOES: Like all interfacings, hair canvas provides strength, body, and support in key areas of garment construction, as on the inside of the hem of a skirt.

WHY USE IT: If tailoring a jacket, using hair canvas in the lapels, for example, is a way to ensure crisp, firm results.

BUCKRAM

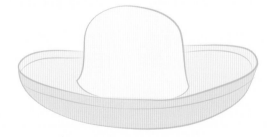

WHAT IT IS: A stiff cloth, typically made from cotton or linen, and used mostly for hat making.

WHAT IT DOES: Millinery buckram is treated with starch so that it can be soaked with water and formed to mold over a hat block to create the main structure.

WHY USE IT: For firm hats, buckram is essential for creating a solid base that will support the rest of the hat.

DOUBLE-FACED RIBBON

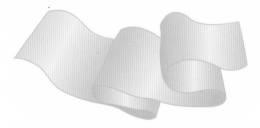

WHAT IT IS: A ribbon of varying content where both sides of the ribbon are equally finished and there is no "wrong" side.

WHAT IT DOES: It looks beautiful from all angles, unlike single-faced ribbon or woven ribbon, which both have a "right" and "wrong" side.

WHY USE IT: Double-faced ribbon is best if you are using a ribbon in a spot where all sides will be visible. It is especially luxurious and works well as a waist sash or hair bow.

SINGLE-FACED RIBBON

WHAT IT IS: A decorative trim typically made of synthetic fibers with one shiny, polished "right" side and a dull "wrong" side.

WHAT IT DOES: It provides embellishment when only one side of the trim will be visible, such as when sewn to hems, necklines, and on accessories.

WHY USE IT: If only one side of the ribbon is being shown, single-faced ribbon can be a less expensive alternative to double-faced ribbon. It is also ideal for printed ribbon as the synthetic fibers provide a slightly firmer and more stable surface to print on.

BIAS TAPE

WHAT IT IS: Strips of fabric of varying widths that are cut on the true bias at a 45-degree angle. Typically they are single or double folded.

WHAT IT DOES: It is applied to necklines, hems, and other areas of construction for both decorative detailing and for finishing raw edges.

WHY USE IT: Because the bias of a fabric has the most stretch, bias tape can be pressed into nearly any shape, including a tight curve, so it is ideal for finishing armholes, necklines, and curved hems.

BIAS TAPE MAKER

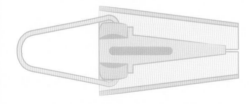

WHAT IT IS: A small handheld tool available in a variety of sizes that assists in the making of bias tape strips.

WHAT IT DOES: Pre-cut bias strips are fed into the large opening at one end, and then come out of the opposite end with the long edges having been folded in. You press the tape in place as it exits the maker, creating single-fold bias tape.

WHY USE IT: Although the same result can be achieved by hand, this tool offers a shortcut by folding the first two folds for you. You can then press the tape in half lengthwise to create double-fold bias tape.

PIPING

WHAT IT IS: Flat piping is a small strip of bias-cut fabric. Corded piping is the same as flat piping, but it is filled with cording for a rounded trim.

WHAT IT DOES: Piping gives visual interest and a decorative touch to any seam, hem, or neckline.

WHY USE IT: Using piping on a project with interesting seam lines can emphasize the way the pieces come together and can make a big impact, especially when used with a solid fabric background.

CORDING

WHAT IT IS: A piece of rope usually made of satin or silk, of any size, that is used in the construction of corded piping or sewn as a decorative trim.

WHAT IT DOES: When making corded piping, unfolded strips of bias-cut fabric are wrapped around a cord and stitched down near the edge of the cording. When used for decorative purposes it is hand sewn to garments as trim.

WHY USE IT: Cording offers a versatile way to customize and embellish projects with fine detailing that can elevate even the humble throw pillow.

NOTIONS

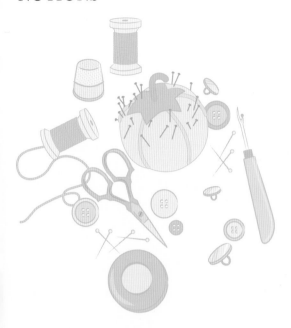

WHAT THEY ARE: This term refers to all of the items, apart from fabric, that are required to complete a project.

WHAT THEY DO: Notions are items like zippers, elastic, buttons, trims, bias tape, and similar objects that are used to embellish, close openings, gather, hem, and complement the fabric.

WHY USE THEM: Some notions (such as trims) are optional, but most are essential to completing a project—especially garments, where notions such as zippers and buttons are critical in the construction process.

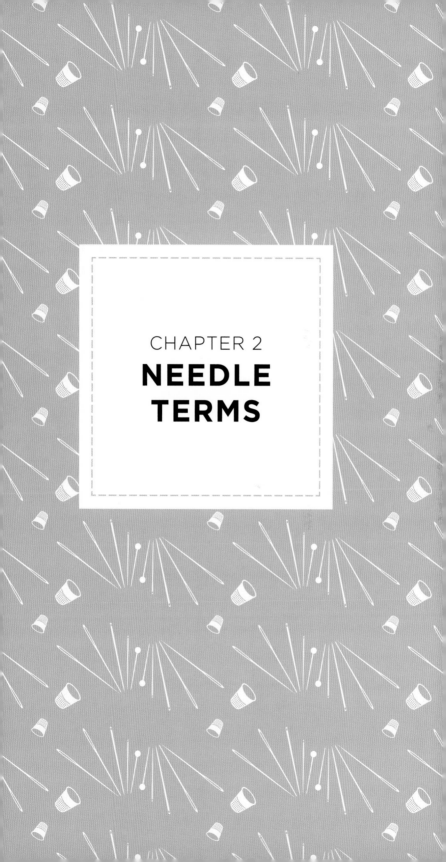

CHAPTER 2
NEEDLE
TERMS

UNIVERSAL NEEDLE

WHAT IT IS: A sewing-machine needle with an average point at the end.

WHAT IT DOES: The all-purpose point allows the needle to be used on both knit and woven fabrics, as it will most likely penetrate the fabric without breaking any threads.

WHY USE IT: If you need to stock a general needle in your sewing studio, this is a good choice. However, it is always better to purchase a fabric-specific needle when you have the opportunity.

MICROTEX SHARP NEEDLE

WHAT IT IS: A sewing-machine needle with a fine and very sharp point.

WHAT IT DOES: The sharp point of the needle pierces through the threads of woven fabric without breaking any fibers.

WHY USE IT: It is always best to pair the fabric being used with an appropriate needle, as the design of each needle is specific to the fabric content and weave. The Microtex sharp is best used for woven fabrics.

BALL-POINT NEEDLE

WHAT IT IS: A sewing machine needle with a slightly rounded tip.

WHAT IT DOES: The rounded tip allows the point of the needle to glide gently between the threads of knit, jersey, and stretch fabrics while being sewn with the sewing machine.

WHY USE IT: The ball-point needle will prevent any accidental thread breakage during the sewing process, keeping the knit weave of the fabric intact so a hole doesn't develop and unravel.

WEDGE-POINT NEEDLE

WHAT IT IS: A sewing-machine needle that has a beveled shaft just above the point.

WHAT IT DOES: The sharp bevel pierces through heavy fibers and non-fiber materials, like leather and vinyl.

WHY USE IT: A needle with a smooth, tapered shaft will not have the same force as a needle that is designed with a wedge point, making it an ideal choice for thick materials.

TWIN NEEDLE

WHAT IT IS: A sewing-machine needle with two needles coming off of the same base, both with eyes near the points.

WHAT IT DOES: A twin needle requires two spools of thread and both needles will stitch simultaneously, creating two lines of stitching at the same time, with a zigzag stitch on the underside.

WHY USE IT: Twin-needle stitches are often used for decorative detailing. They also provide a great way to hem stretch fabrics with a conventional sewing machine, as the threads allow the fabric to stretch when pulled.

NEEDLE ANATOMY

SHAFT

WHAT IT IS: The part of a sewing-machine needle between the shank and the eye.

WHAT IT DOES: The diameter of the needle's shaft determines the size of the needle.

WHY USE IT: It is always critical to use the correct sized needle for the project you are sewing, so check the size of the shaft to match a fine fabric with a smaller needle, and vice versa.

SHANK

WHAT IT IS: The uppermost part of a sewing-machine needle. Home-machine needles have a shank with one flat side and one rounded side.

WHAT IT DOES: The shank's shape allows it to be inserted into the machine correctly every time.

WHY USE IT: If you plan to sew with a sewing machine instead of by hand, the needle is a critical element. While many needles are universal, make sure the shank of the needle you purchased will work in your brand of machine.

EYE

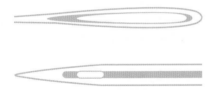

WHAT IT IS: On a hand-sewing needle, the eye is the open hole at the opposite end to the point (top). On a sewing-machine needle, the eye is the open hole at the same end as the point (bottom).

WHAT IT DOES: The thread feeds through the eye of the needle during the sewing process.

WHY USE IT: Quite simply, nothing will be sewn if the eye of your needle is not threaded!

GROOVE

WHAT IT IS: An indentation down the center of the shaft of a sewing-machine needle.

WHAT IT DOES: The thread feeds down the needle, nesting itself into the groove of the needle as it passes to the eye at the bottom.

WHY USE IT: When threaded properly, the thread will automatically place itself into the groove and remain there while in use.

POINT

WHAT IT IS: The part of a sewing-machine needle located between the eye and the tip.

WHAT IT DOES: Each needle's point and tip are sized and shaped according to the size and type of needle.

WHY USE IT: It is very important to use the correct point and tip for the content of the fabric you are working with. Knits require a rounded tip, while wovens prefer a sharp point and tip.

CALYX

WHAT IT IS: A sewing needle with a very small split opening in the eye.

WHAT IT DOES: The split in a calyx allows the needle's eye to be threaded with great ease.

WHY USE IT: Ideal for people with less than perfect eyesight, a calyx needle can be threaded by sliding the thread along the needle into the split, instead of threading directly through the eye.

DOLL

WHAT IT IS: A very long needle used mostly in the hand sewing of dolls.

WHAT IT DOES: The length of the needle allows you to sew and apply facial features with precision.

WHY USE IT: For fine detailing, a long and thin needle will give you greater control when sewing through the body of a doll.

SHARPS

WHAT THEY ARE: Hand-sewing needles with a very sharp, thin point, available in sizes I to I2.

WHAT THEY DO: Sharps are slightly longer than other needles and are used in quilting, garment construction, hand appliqué, quilt binding, and many other tasks.

WHY USE THEM: Sharps are the most universal, all-purpose needle to have on hand and are available in multisized packs to suit a range of situations.

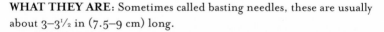 **SEE ALSO**: Appliqué, page I75

LONGS

WHAT THEY ARE: Sometimes called basting needles, these are usually about 3–3¹/₂ in (7.5–9 cm) long.

WHAT THEY DO: Often used in quilting, longs are frequently used when hand basting during garment construction, or when preparing a fabric pieces for quilting.

WHY USE THEM: Their length speeds up the process of basting by hand as you can load a handful of stitches on the needle before pulling it through, as with a running stitch.

 SEE ALSO: Basting stitch, page 78; Baste, page 87

BETWEENS/QUILTING NEEDLES

WHAT THEY ARE: These are short, strong hand-sewing needles, available in a range of sizes.

WHAT THEY DO: Their short size and small eye aid in hand sewing as they can be pushed through multiple layers of fabric.

WHY USE THEM: Hand quilting is a long and committed task, so having a needle that will pass through layers with ease will make the process an enjoyable one.

 SEE ALSO: Quilting, page 88

CHENILLE

WHAT IT IS: A large hand-sewing needle with a large eye and a sharp point.

WHAT IT DOES: The large eye allows for thicker threads, embroidery floss, and ribbons to be sewn by hand.

WHY USE IT: Sewing with thicker threads can be very difficult when the needle's eye is too small for easy threading. The eye of a chenille needle allows you to get creative with your embellishment choices.

CURVED NEEDLE

WHAT IT IS: A hand-sewing needle with an eye at one end and a point at the opposite end, which is curved into a semicircle.

WHAT IT DOES: It allows you to sew in tight situations where curving up or down is easier than sewing straight.

WHY USE IT: Available in a range of sizes, curved needles will aid in sewing everything from upholstery to applying beads to a gown.

TAPESTRY NEEDLE

WHAT IT IS: Much like a chenille, a tapestry needle is a hand-sewing needle that is blunt and strong, with a large eye.

WHAT IT DOES: Because of its strength, it is often used when making tapestries, sewing with thicker embellishments, or in crochet and yarn crafts.

WHY USE IT: When working with thicker fibers, the large eye will prove helpful during threading, and the strength of the needle will prevent bending during sewing.

 SEE ALSO: Seams, page 168

PUNCH NEEDLE

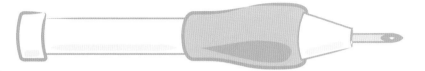

WHAT IT IS: A hand-sewing tool with a handle at one end and an eye at the other. It is threaded through the handle.

WHAT IT DOES: When you "punch" this needle through fabric, it leaves a loop of thread behind, allowing you to essentially "draw" with the tool.

WHY USE IT: For a nice alternative to embroidery, needle punching is a fun way to embellish fabric.

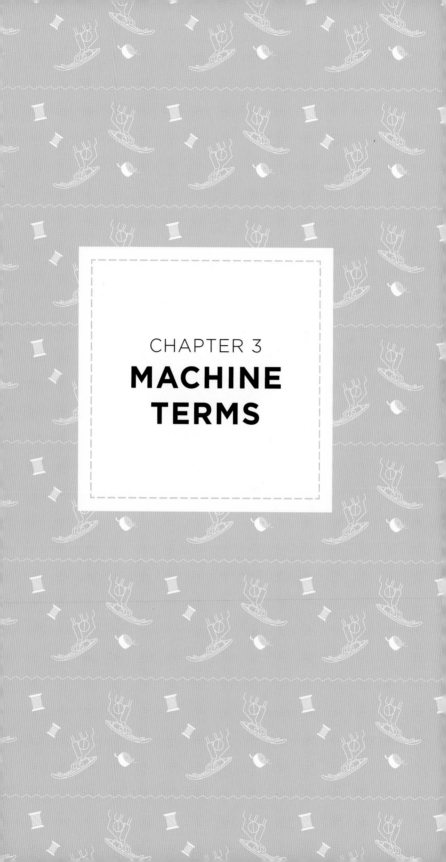

CHAPTER 3
MACHINE TERMS

HANDWHEEL

WHAT IT IS: A large dial on the right side of the sewing machine that moves around as the machine stitches forward and backward.

WHAT IT DOES: When the handwheel turns toward you, that is the motion of sewing. The handwheel will move as the machine sews, or it can be turned manually.

WHY USE IT: When sewing with the machine, you do not have to consider the handwheel. But when finishing a stitch, or moving forward or backward manually, this is the best way to ensure single stitches. It is also helpful to move manually when sewing over thick areas.

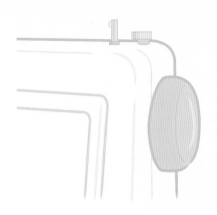

PEDAL

WHAT IT IS: The pedal is attached to the sewing machine with an electrical cord. It sits on the floor and supplies power to the machine.

WHAT IT DOES: The pedal often has a narrow end and a wider end. Place the pedal under the foot with the narrow (or hinged) side facing you and place your foot on top. The speed of the machine is controlled by how much the pedal is pushed.

WHY USE IT: The handwheel can be used for single manual stitches, but most sewing is done with the assistance of the pedal.

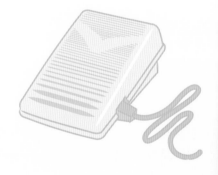

DISPLAY

WHAT IT IS: A digital or computerized screen on the face of the sewing machine, usually near the stitch length, stitch width, and stitch selector dials.

WHAT IT DOES: This will display a host of things, depending on your machine's make and model, but most often it indicates the stitch selected, as well as its length and width settings.

WHY USE IT: If your model has a display, there is no avoiding using it, as it will be front and center on your machine. If there is no display, that means your machine is mechanical, with no computer or electronic controls.

STITCH SELECTOR

WHAT IT IS: A button, dial, knob, or digital screen on the face of the sewing machine with a diagram of stitch options.

WHAT IT DOES: This device allows you to choose from the variety of stitches offered by the machine.

WHY USE IT: Machines come in many varieties, from those with only one stitch choice, to those with hundreds of options. Being able to select the stitch best suited for your project is key to success and if the machine has many choices, you will inevitably use more than one along the way.

REVERSE BUTTON

WHAT IT IS: A button, usually located at the lower right of the machine, or just above the needle area, that moves the machine in reverse.

WHAT IT DOES: When the reverse button is engaged, the sewing machine sews the selected stitch in reverse.

WHY USE IT: Sewing a backstitch at the start and end of any straight stitch will ensure that the stitches stay locked in place.

PRESSER FOOT

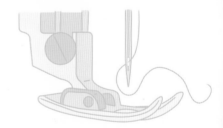

WHAT IT IS: A small metal or plastic attachment that the needle passes between before it pierces the fabric beneath.

WHAT IT DOES: When lowered onto the fabric prior to sewing, the presser foot holds the fabric in place on top of the feed dogs. The fabric is then fed through the machine.

WHY USE IT: A sewing machine cannot be properly operated without a presser foot. There are many basic and complex feet available for every make and model of sewing machine, each with a different purpose.

THROAT PLATE

WHAT IT IS: Underneath the presser foot is a metal square that houses the feed dogs and the seam allowance measurements. This is the throat plate.

WHAT IT DOES: All sewing takes place on top of this plate. It is the gathering point for the needle, fabric, seam allowance measurements, feed dogs, and the bobbin thread.

WHY USE IT: You cannot avoid the throat plate during the sewing process, and it is a critical junction for a multitude of tasks.

FEED DOGS

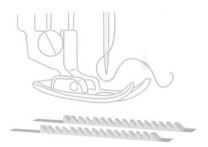

WHAT THEY ARE: Small metal teeth that live under the presser foot and poke above the throat plate.

WHAT THEY DO: These teeth pull fabric through the machine using a rotating motion—gliding back, sinking into the machine, coming forward, popping up through the throat plate, and gliding back again. This motion is repeated over and over, at the speed dictated by how much the pedal is pushed.

WHY USE THEM: Do not resist the pull of the teeth, or try to push the fabric through faster—letting the feed dogs pull the fabric through the machine will ensure even stitching.

SEAM ALLOWANCE MEASUREMENTS

WHAT THEY ARE: Measurement marks written or etched into the throat plate, under the presser foot. Some machines include numbers; others simply feature lines.

WHAT THEY DO: When the needle is in the central position, these provide a guide for achieving specific seam allowances. So when the edge of the fabric is up against the ⁵⁄₈-in (1.5-cm) mark, the resulting stitch will be ⁵⁄₈ in (1.5 cm) from the fabric's edge.

WHY USE THEM: The correct seam allowance ensures your pieces line up properly, and result in the desired size at the end of the project.

TAKE-UP LEVER

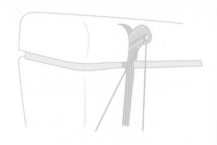

WHAT IT IS: A metal loop that the thread passes through between the tension and the eye of the needle.

WHAT IT DOES: The take-up lever helps feed the thread through the machine, and is also an indicator of where you are in relation to the start and finish of your stitch.

WHY USE IT: When finishing a stitch, check the lever to see if it is raised in its highest position. If not, turn the handwheel toward you to finish the stitch so that the thread and fabric come out of the machine with ease.

VERTICAL SPOOL PIN

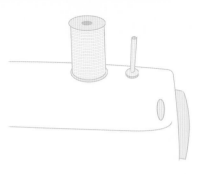

WHAT IT IS: A piece of plastic or metal on the top of your sewing machine near the bobbin winder.

WHAT IT DOES: The upright stick is threaded through the open center of a spool of thread. From here the machine is threaded for sewing.

WHY USE IT: Often a vertical spool pin can be used in lieu of a horizontal spool pin to allow you to sew with specialty fibers, or cone thread originally intended for serger/overlock machines.

 SEE ALSO: Cone thread, page 20; Serger/Overlocker, page 73

HORIZONTAL SPOOL PIN

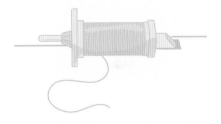

WHAT IT IS: A piece of plastic or metal with a small stopper located on the top of the sewing machine. This sits horizontally, with a cavity beneath it.

WHAT IT DOES: The stick part of the spool pin is threaded through a spool of thread, and the stopper holds the thread in place on the pin while the machine is in use.

WHY USE IT: The function of a machine is engineered based on the thread path, stemming from the spool pin. To ensure proper sewing, use the included spool pin instead of locating the thread anywhere else.

TENSION

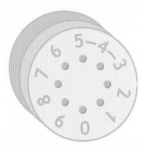

WHAT IT IS: A pair of round metal disks that are housed behind a dial on the face of the machine.

WHAT IT DOES: When the presser foot is lowered, the metal disks are engaged and it is the tension's job to evenly distribute the thread, based on the setting on the tension dial.

WHY USE IT: For general sewing on medium, lightweight, and slightly heavyweight fabrics, the tension can usually be turned to the recommended number by the manufacturer. Only when working with extremely light or heavy fabrics should this dial be moved.

BOBBIN

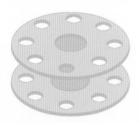

WHAT IT IS: A circular piece of metal or plastic with two levels and a shaft between the two.

WHAT IT DOES: A bobbin is the second spool of thread that it takes to form a stitch. The bobbin lives in the bobbin case under the presser foot and forms the underside of each stitch.

WHY USE IT: Your machine may move, but nothing will actually stitch without both the spool of thread and bobbin in position in the machine.

BOBBIN WINDER

WHAT IT IS: A small metal or plastic knob on the sewing machine that the bobbin fits onto.

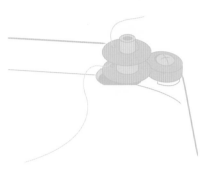

WHAT IT DOES: The bobbin winder is how you transfer thread from the spool to the bobbin.

WHY USE IT: It is important to read your machine's manual on how to thread the machine for proper bobbin winding; if it has incorrect tension during the winding, the stitch will not sew correctly.

BOBBIN CASE

WHAT IT IS: The housing under the presser foot where the bobbin sits during sewing.

WHAT IT DOES: For proper threading and stitching, each element of the machine must be in place, and this is where the bobbin is designed to be.

WHY USE IT: The bobbin is sized to fit into the case and feed thread into the stitch based on the tension set by the tiny screw on the bobbin case. This will ensure a perfect stitch.

DROP-IN BOBBIN

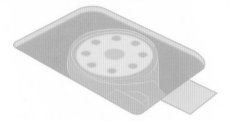

WHAT IT IS: A space directly under the presser foot that is accessed with an opening in the throat plate where the bobbin sits during sewing.

WHAT IT DOES: Machines are designed to have either a drop-in bobbin or a front-loading bobbin, and the thread feeds from that point to the stitch at the needle.

WHY USE IT: If your machine has a drop-in bobbin, one benefit is that you can often see it during sewing, which in turn allows you to see if you are running low on thread.

SPECIALTY MACHINES

LONG-ARM QUILTER

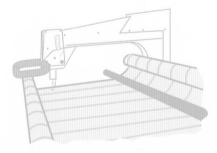

WHAT IT IS: A sewing machine with a longer distance than usual between the needle and the body.

WHAT IT DOES: This larger space allows you to fit larger quantities of fabric into the machine.

WHY USE IT: When quilting or working on larger projects, more fabric than usual needs to fit in the small space between the needle and the body, and this makes that much easier.

SERGER/OVERLOCKER

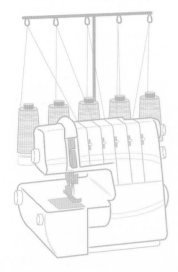

WHAT IT IS: A sewing machine that sews with two to five cone threads.

WHAT IT DOES: The threads of this machine stitch one to two straight construction stitches while the remaining threads loop around the raw edge of the fabric, which is cut by the machine's internal knife at your preferred seam allowance.

WHY USE IT: Many commercial garments are sewn with a serger, as it provides a professional finish on the inside of a project.

 SEE ALSO: Serging/Overlocking, page 84

CHAPTER 4
STITCH
TERMS

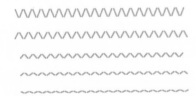

MACHINE STITCHES

STITCH LENGTH

WHAT IT IS: The length of a stitch—from where it begins to where it ends—as set by the sewing machine or when stitching by hand.

WHAT IT DOES: The length of a stitch can determine if it is meant for construction purposes or for decorative use.

WHY USE IT: The length of any stitch must always be predetermined, based on the type of stitch and its intended application.

STITCH WIDTH

WHAT IT IS: The width of a stitch from side to side of center, as set by the sewing machine or when stitching by hand.

WHAT IT DOES: A straight stitch does not have width, but most other stitches do.

WHY USE IT: As with stitch length, this is a required element in every stitch, and is determined by its use and placement. Even if stitch width is set to zero, this needs to be considered before beginning the sewing process.

STRAIGHT STITCH

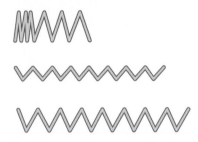

WHAT IT IS: A series of single stitches, with each one starting where the last finished, for a continuous line.

WHAT IT DOES: When two or more pieces of fabric are stitched with a straight stitch, it forms a seam. It also creates a smooth line for decorative purposes.

WHY USE IT: A straight stitch is used to sew construction seams, to decorate with topstitching, to sew basting stitches, to create a backstitch, and for many more practical situations.

ZIGZAG STITCH

WHAT IT IS: A Z-shaped stitch that is formed by sewing alternately to the right of center, then to the left of center.

WHAT IT DOES: This creates a slightly stretchy stitch; it also has decorative applications. It also can be used to "wrap" thread around a fabric edge.

WHY USE IT: Zigzag stitches are a good alternative to stretch stitches when sewing with knit fabrics. Wrapping zigzag threads around a raw edge can provide seam finishing and prevent a fabric from fraying.

STRETCH STITCH

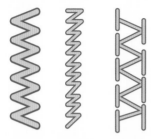

WHAT IT IS: A stretch version of common machine stitches, like straight stitch, blind hem, and zigzag.

WHAT IT DOES: Each version of a stretch stitch moves forward a few stitches, then reverses a single stitch to provide a stretch in the stitch itself.

WHY USE IT: When sewing with knit fabrics that stretch, the stitch must stretch as well or the threads will snap when pulled. A stretch stitch will stretch with the fabric.

BASTING STITCH

WHAT IT IS: A straight stitch with a very long length, 4.0 mm or longer.

WHAT IT DOES: It is most commonly used for temporarily holding layers together during the construction or fitting process.

WHY USE IT: Perfect to use when sewing a muslin test garment, as you can remove it easily. It is also used when gathering by hand, and easing in pieces during garment construction, such as setting in a sleeve.

BACKSTITCH

WHAT IT IS: Reversing over a straight stitch by a few stitches provides a backstitch, sometimes also called a lockstitch.

WHAT IT DOES: Typically used at the beginning and end of a construction straight stitch, the backstitch prevents the stitching from unraveling.

WHY USE IT: A backstitch is necessary for making sure your stitching stays in place.

DECORATIVE STITCHING

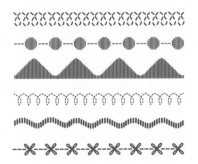

WHAT IT IS: Any non-construction stitching is decorative.

WHAT IT DOES: Provides decoration based on the location and stitch variation used.

WHY USE IT: Everything from topstitching and zigzag stitches to more elaborate programmed stitches and hand stitches can be used as a decorative stitch when sewn on the right side of a project.

SEAM

WHAT IT IS: When two or more pieces of fabric are sewn together, a seam is made.

WHAT IT DOES: It is the basic formation of every intersection on any task.

WHY USE IT: When making nearly any three-dimensional item, a seam will be formed at some point in the process. Determine in advance how all the pieces will fit together to form the seams of your project.

PUCKERING

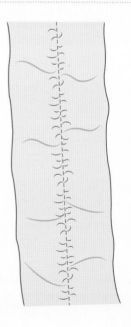

WHAT IT IS: Rippling or pinches in the fabric that may occur during the sewing process.

WHAT IT DOES: If the tension or stitch length on the machine is set incorrectly, or if you are using the wrong size needle for the type of fabric being used, puckering and ripples will appear along the seam.

WHY USE IT: Don't use it! It's important that you test your stitch on a scrap of fabric before sewing the finished garment. Make sure all the elements are set correctly to prevent puckering from happening.

TOPSTITCHING

WHAT IT IS: Similar to edge stitching, but not sewn quite so close to the edge of the finished edge, topstitching is a straight stitch sewn on the right side of a garment, most often at seams and hems.

WHAT IT DOES: Topstitching provides visual interest along construction seams, and is also a quick and easy way to hem the bottom of garments or sleeves.

WHY USE IT: For a slightly more casual finish, topstitching a hem is faster than hand stitching it. Topstitching can also elevate denim pants to look more like commercially made jeans.

EDGE STITCHING

WHAT IT IS: Similar to topstitching, edge stitching is a straight stitch sewn very close to the finished edge of fabric.

WHAT IT DOES: Edge stitching is typically used for utilitarian purposes, and helps to hold or condense multiple layers together.

WHY USE IT: Unlike topstitching, which is mostly decorative, edge stitching tends to be seen more frequently on collars, facings, and in other construction situations.

GARMENT STITCHING

STAY STITCHING

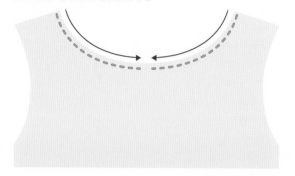

WHAT IT IS: A straight stitch, of a regular or slightly shorter length, which is sewn inside the seam allowance around the curve of a cut pattern piece.

WHAT IT DOES: The threads of the stay stitch help hold the threads of the fabric in place.

WHY USE IT: This quick and easy preventative measure keeps a curved area—such as a neckline—from stretching out of shape during the construction process.

UNDERSTITCH

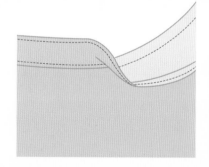

WHAT IT IS: A straight stitch joining the seam allowance of a seam to that same seam's lining or facing, just inside the original seam.

WHAT IT DOES: Attaching the seam allowance to the inside fabric helps roll the facing or lining to just the inside of the seam, securing it in place.

WHY USE IT: Using an understitch keeps the lining or facing out of sight on the right side of the garment for a professional finish.

 SEE ALSO: Facing, page 148; Lining, page 166

EASE STITCHING

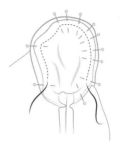

WHAT IT IS: An ease stitch is a basting stitch, with no backstitching at the start or finish.

WHAT IT DOES: It is used for the purpose of easing one larger edge of fabric to fit another slightly smaller edge of fabric.

WHY USE IT: When inserting a set-in sleeve or dealing with a similar situation, ease stitching helps shape the larger piece to fit against the smaller piece, before being pinned and sewn with a final construction stitch.

STITCH IN THE DITCH

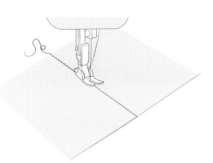

WHAT IT IS: A straight stitch that lands in the groove where two seams meet on the right side of a project.

WHAT IT DOES: Meant to be an invisible stitch, the threads of the straight stitch sink into the seam and tack the right side to an inner layer or lining.

WHY USE IT: Often used on facings or waistbands, stitching in the ditch provides a clean finish instead of using a topstitch that would be entirely visible.

GARMENT STITCHING

SERGING/OVERLOCKING

WHAT IT IS: A serger or overlock stitch cuts off the seam allowance with an internal knife of a serging or overlock sewing machine.

WHAT IT DOES: The 3 to 5 threads of the machine stitch 1 to 2 straight construction stitches while the remaining threads loop around the raw edge of the fabric which is cut by the machine's knife at your set seam allowance.

WHY USE IT: It provides a professional finish on the inside of a project. The stitch's formation also allows threads to stretch, making it ideal for knit fabrics as well.

 SEE ALSO: Serger/Overlocker, page 73

COVER STITCH

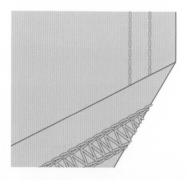

WHAT IT IS: A row of multiple straight stitches on the right side, with a zigzag stitch on the underside.

WHAT IT DOES: A coverstitch creates a stretch stitch for use when hemming knit fabrics.

WHY USE IT: To finish knits with a professional finish, a coverstitch provides a clean finish while also stretching when a garment is pulled on.

BUTTONHOLE STITCH

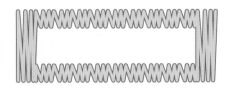

WHAT IT IS: Two rows of short and wide zigzag stitches, with a bar tack stitch at the top and bottom, and a slit cut down the middle.

WHAT IT DOES: The open slit down the middle of the stitches provides an opening for a button to pass through to keep two layers together.

WHY USE IT: A button and buttonhole are common closures for blouses, dresses, jackets, and the top of pants.

BLIND HEM STITCH

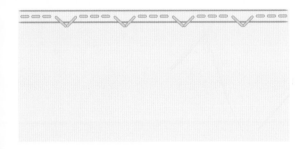

WHAT IT IS: A series of stitches—several small and one large V—that attach a hem to the inside of a garment.

WHAT IT DOES: The uppermost part of the large V stitch creates a small dot on the right side of the garment, while the rest of the stitches are attached to the hem alone.

WHY USE IT: The blind hem stitch provides a near invisible hem for a much more elegant finish than a topstitch.

RUNNING STITCH

WHAT IT IS: A straight stitch sewn by hand, where dashes with gaps between them show on both sides of the fabric.

WHAT IT DOES: A running stitch is sewn by layering multiple stitches onto the needle, then pulling through, making three to four stitches at a time.

WHY USE IT: Often used as a basting stitch for fabrics that are delicate, such as silk or velvet, it can also be used for decorative detailing.

PRICKSTITCH

WHAT IT IS: A hand stitch where long threads are left on the wrong side and small dots are left on the right side of the fabric.

WHAT IT DOES: Provides minimal visibility of the stitch on the right side of the garment while still providing structure.

WHY USE IT: A prickstitch is commonly used to insert a zipper by hand, or when sewing fabrics that will potentially be damaged if put through the sewing machine, such as velvet.

BASTE

WHAT IT IS: A straight stitch with a longer than average length, sewn by hand or by machine.

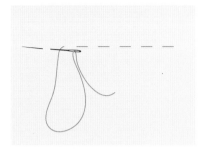

WHAT IT DOES: A baste stitch is a temporary stitch, used to hold two things together during the construction process. The baste stitch will never show on the right side of a finished item—it is removed or hidden inside the seam allowance.

WHY USE IT: Most commonly used during fittings, when gathering by hand, or to ease two pieces together.

 SEE ALSO: Gathering, page 141; Longs, page 58

FLAT CATCH STITCH

WHAT IT IS: A series of X-shaped hand stitches.

WHAT IT DOES: A flat catch stitch joins two pieces of fabric together, while allowing them to remain flat on top of each other, or side by side, instead of overlapping.

WHY USE IT: Often found in lining applications, it is great to use when a flat and invisible joining is required, but added bulk is not desired.

OVERCAST STITCH

WHAT IT IS: A hand stitch where thread is wrapped around the raw edge of one or more pieces of fabric.

WHAT IT DOES: The wrapped thread prevents the threads of the fabric from unraveling when washed, dried, and worn.

WHY USE IT: The same end result can be achieved with the use of a zigzag stitch or serger stitch, but doing an overcast stitch by hand is an elegant and more couture approach to seam finishing.

 SEE ALSO: Serging/Overlocking, page 84; Zigzag stitch, page 77

QUILTING

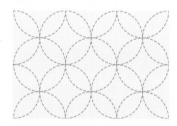

WHAT IT IS: A quilting stitch is a hand-sewn stitch with a series of small dots or dashes on either side of the quilt top and backing.

WHAT IT DOES: This stitch joins the layers of the quilt and the interior batting and holds them in place.

WHY USE IT: The hand stitching provides a necessary stability for the layers of the quilt. Alternatively, you can quilt the layers together with a straight stitch on the sewing machine.

 SEE ALSO: Quilting, page 186

HEMMING STITCH

WHAT IT IS: A hand stitch that joins the inside of a hem to the fabric above it.

WHAT IT DOES: The stitch is sewn through the top of the hem, through a very small amount of the main garment, then through the hem.

WHY USE IT: Much like a machine blind hem, this leaves only a very small dot of thread on the right side of the garment, creating a clean and professional finish for more formal items.

DARNING

WHAT IT IS: A method of repairing a hole in a piece of fabric or finished garment.

WHAT IT DOES: A series of hand stitches are sewn in a variety of directions to strengthen the fabric and repair a hole.

WHY USE IT: If a loved garment has developed a hole, this is the best way to repair it and continue to love it instead of tossing it out.

TACK

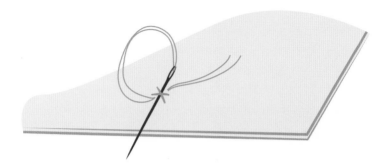

WHAT IT IS: A stitch made by hand sewing with long running stitches or single tack spots.

WHAT IT DOES: Tailor's tacks are used to mark construction details like darts, and running tack stitches are much like baste stitches, which mimic the final stitching but are only intended to be temporary.

WHY USE IT: If marking on the fabric with a writing tool will damage the fabric, tacks are often used instead.

TAILOR'S KNOT

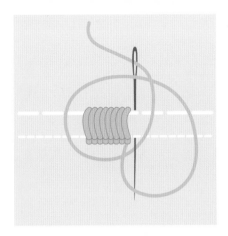

WHAT IT IS: A method of knotting thread while threaded through a hand-sewing needle.

WHAT IT DOES: By forming a loop with the thread, then feeding the needle and thread back through the loop and forming a knot, this provides an easy way to knot off at the end of anything that involves hand stitching.

WHY USE IT: Perfect for use when sewing on buttons—this is a strong and clean way to finish with a knot.

CHAPTER 5
FABRIC
TERMS

WARP

WHAT IT IS: The threads that run the length of a woven fabric.

WHAT IT DOES: The warp threads are wrapped with firm tension onto the loom in preparation of being woven into fabric.

WHY USE IT: Woven fabrics are commonly used in sewing, and all woven fabrics consist of a set of warp and weft threads, making them a very stable choice for projects.

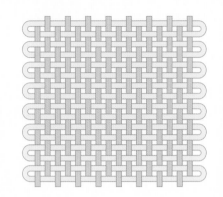

WEFT

WHAT IT IS: The threads that run the width of fabric when woven.

WHAT IT DOES: The weft threads are woven into the warp in a variety of ways, sliding above and below the warp threads, going back and forth from side to side.

WHY USE IT: Weft threads are one of the important building blocks in woven fabrics—they create the pattern and weave style of a particular fabric.

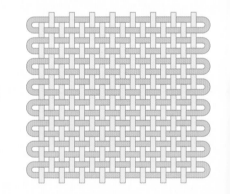

GRAIN

WHAT IT IS: The threads that run the length of the fabric (the warp) form the grain.

WHAT IT DOES: Every pattern piece features a grainline indication to guide you when placing it "on grain"—parallel with the grain of the fabric.

WHY USE IT: Pieces must be cut parallel with the grain of the fabric for the final garment to fit and drape properly. If this step is missed, the pieces will not fit together, fit your body, or stretch and hang correctly.

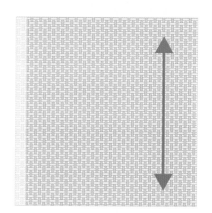

CROSSGRAIN

WHAT IT IS: The threads that run the width of the fabric (the weft).

WHAT IT DOES: The crossgrain is woven looser than the grain, and therefore retains more stretch. This stretch is typically designed to fit around the body so that the little bit of stretch it provides eases with the wearing of a garment.

WHY USE IT: As with grain, it is critical to the construction and fit of a garment that pattern pieces are placed correctly on the crossgrain of the fabric.

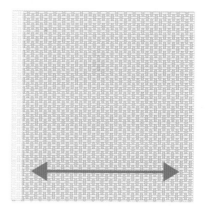

OFF GRAIN

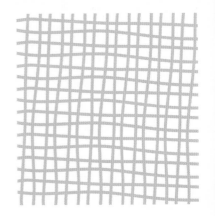

WHAT IT IS: When the threads of the warp and weft of fabric are not sitting perfectly perpendicular with each other.

WHAT IT DOES: If a pattern piece is cut off grain, then it will not fold, sew, press, or fit as the designer intended.

WHY USE IT: Making sure your fabric is folded on grain prior to cutting any pattern piece, and placing each pattern piece with the grain, will ensure perfect fit and predictable behavior from the fabric.

SELVAGE

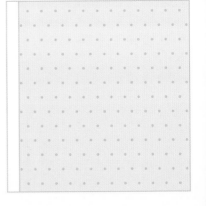

WHAT IT IS: The self-finished edge of a piece of fabric, where the weft doubles back on the fabric.

WHAT IT DOES: The selvage prevents fabric from unraveling and fraying, and also provides the printer a place to mark the fabric with the designer's name, print name and collection, as well as print test marks for color verification.

WHY USE IT: When sewing, you usually cut off the selvage, because the finished edges will wash, shrink, and wear at a different rate than the rest of the cloth. This might then result in a warped drape in the finished project.

RIGHT SIDE

WHAT IT IS: The right side of fabric is the side that will be shown and worn on the outside of the finished project.

WHAT IT DOES: Prints that are formed from woven threads have no right or wrong side, but printed fabrics or those with a nap have a clear right side that is to be displayed on the outside.

WHY USE IT: To show off your beautiful fabric, of course!

 SEE ALSO: Nap, page 121

WRONG SIDE

WHAT IT IS: The wrong side of fabric is the underside, which will be hidden on the inside of your finished project.

WHAT IT DOES: On printed fabric or fabric with nap, the wrong side is very clear as it is the side without image or texture. On fabrics where the print is woven, there is often no right or wrong side.

WHY USE IT: The wrong side is where all your construction marking is made, so use it to your advantage.

BIAS

WHAT IT IS: The bias is the 45-degree angle that runs diagonally across a piece of fabric.

WHAT IT DOES: The bias is the most stretchy and fluid part of a fabric, making the resulting drape quite different than that produced when cut on the warp or the weft.

WHY USE IT: As the bias has great stretch, this can be used to the designer's advantage, since the fabric will hang in a more graceful way across the body.

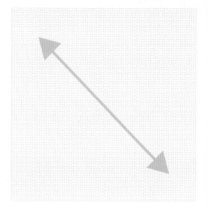

DRAPE

WHAT IT IS: The fluidity of the way a fabric hangs.

WHAT IT DOES: The drape of a fabric can dramatically influence the finished outcome of a project— a stiffer fabric will not hang in the same way as a flowy fabric.

WHY USE IT: Pairing a project with a fabric that has an appropriate drape is important. Something with gathers will be better served by something drapey, whereas pleats can handle something crisper, and with less drape.

FIBER CONTENT

WHAT IT IS: The content and source material of a fabric.

WHAT IT DOES: This includes where the fibers originated, how they were manufactured and dyed, and details about the raw materials that make up the fabric. Content can be determined with a burn test.

WHY USE IT: Understanding different fibers—say, whether they contain stretch elements, or come from natural or man-made sources— is key to choosing the correct fabric. For example, if a project requires heavy pressing, natural fibers will be the best choice, since man-made fibers can melt under extreme heat.

BLEND

WHAT IT IS: A blend implies that the fabric content is made up of more than one type of fiber, as is often used in active wear.

WHAT IT DOES: Depending on the fabric, a blend is often a combination of a man-made fiber and a natural fiber to provide stretch, drape, or washability.

WHY USE IT: As with any project and fabric pairing, matching the fabric content to a project is important. Knowing, for example, that the cotton fabric you have picked has spandex included for stretch will greatly influence the end result.

COTTON

WHAT IT IS: A plant that produces large, fluffy "balls" of white fiber. This is harvested and spun into thread, and woven to become fabric.

WHAT IT DOES: This is a natural fiber that is available in a variety of fabric weights, depending on the thickness of the spun threads.

WHY USE IT: Cotton is the most widely available fiber. When woven into fabric, it is breathable, durable, and easy to care for, so a popular choice for a wide range of projects. It is also easy to print on, making it a great base for printed fabrics.

HEMP

WHAT IT IS: A fiber sourced from the stem of the cannabis plant. This is spun into thread, and woven to become fabric.

WHAT IT DOES: Hemp is a natural fiber that, like cotton, can be made into a wide range of weights to create a strong natural fabric.

WHY USE IT: If you require a medium-weight to heavyweight breathable fabric, hemp is a good choice. It is usually found in its natural color, or dyed into solid colors with natural dyes.

LINEN

WHAT IT IS: A fiber sourced from the stem of the flax plant. The fibers are spun into thread and then woven to become fabric.

WHAT IT DOES: Linen is a widely used natural fiber and is woven into superfine, featherweight fabric as well as heavy canvas.

WHY USE IT: This complex fabric is both drapey and stiff at the same time. It retains its wrinkles, which means it is also a great choice for garments that feature pressed details, such as pleats and tucks.

SILK

WHAT IT IS: A fiber sourced from the cocoon produced by the silk moth caterpillar. It is spun into thread and woven to become fabric.

WHAT IT DOES: Since the fiber source is extra fine, the thread made from silk is thin, and can be woven to create fluid, elegant fabric.

WHY USE IT: When working with a project that requires tremendous drape, silk is an excellent choice, as it is also a breathable natural fabric.

RAYON

WHAT IT IS: A semi-synthetic fiber made by chemically converting wood pulp into thread. It is then woven into fabric.

WHAT IT DOES: Rayon is chemically treated to become a lightweight, drapey fabric, as well as a variety of knits, such as rayon jersey, viscose, and modal.

WHY USE IT: When you would like the drape of silk but would prefer something easier to care for, rayon is a great choice.

ALPACA WOOL

WHAT IT IS: Alpaca fleece shorn from the animal, then spun and woven into a wool fabric.

WHAT IT DOES: Alpaca is free from lanolin (the wax found in other types of wool), making it a soft, warm, and hypoallergenic alternative to wool.

WHY USE IT: When wanting a non-sheep version of wool, alpaca offers the same variety of weights and colors for a wide range of projects.

MUSLIN

WHAT IT IS: An undyed or bleached fabric available in a wide range of weights. It is made from cotton fibers with a plain weave.

WHAT IT DOES: What was once used in dressmaking is now mostly used as a blank canvas for making test garments—or "muslins."

WHY USE IT: When you make a muslin in a weight close to the final fabric for your project, this garment can offer you insights into the fit of the finished garment, and how flattering it will be.

CANVAS

WHAT IT IS: A heavyweight fabric made from natural fibers with a plain weave.

WHAT IT DOES: Because of its durability, canvas is the perfect fabric for totes, bags, and jackets.

WHY USE IT: Canvas offers a strong and breathable product. Water-resistant varieties are also available for making tents, sails, and clothing.

WEAVE

WHAT IT IS: The weave of a fabric refers to the way in which the threads from the warp and the weft are woven together.

WHAT IT DOES: Depending on the pattern, the weave will change the face of the fabric, as seen with drill, twill, and double gauze.

WHY USE IT: Understanding the weave will help you guess how the fabric will behave, drape, wash, and potentially shrink, so that you can make an educated choice when pairing fabric with project.

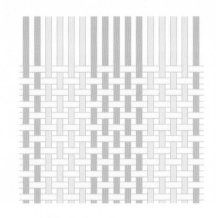

 SEE ALSO: Warp, page 94; Weft, page 94

PLAIN WEAVE

WHAT IT IS: The most basic type of weave on a woven textile.

WHAT IT DOES: Each warp and weft thread crosses the other, one thread at a time, in a straight, crisscross grid pattern.

WHY USE IT: Many woven fabrics have a plain weave, as it is the easiest to make and to print on.

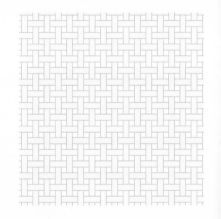

TWILL

WHAT IT IS: A weave style with parallel ribs that travel diagonally down the fabric.

WHAT IT DOES: The diagonal ribbing is formed by passing a weft thread over one or more of the warp threads, then under two or more of the warp threads, creating rows in a diagonal composition.

WHY USE IT: The weave structure can provide interesting patterns based on the color of the threads used, as well as a nice drape.

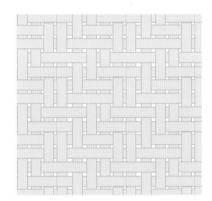

BASKET WEAVE

WHAT IT IS: A plain-weave style of fabric, with a texture like that of a woven basket.

WHAT IT DOES: Each warp and weft pass is made of two threads instead of one in each direction, and the sets of two threads are woven as one unit to create the basket effect.

WHY USE IT: Basket-weave fabrics can be found in both heavyweight upholstery and loose sweater-like yardage. All benefit from the attractive weave structure.

SATIN WEAVE

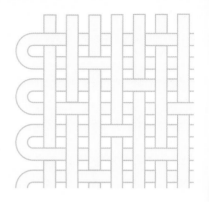

WHAT IT IS: A plain-weave style of fabric that has a shiny right side and a flat wrong side. Satin weaves are usually made from silk or polyester threads.

WHAT IT DOES: A satin weave is created when four or more warp threads float over the weft threads, or vice versa, creating a warp-faced or weft-faced satin respectively.

WHY USE IT: The face of the fabric is elegant and perfect for finer garments and intimate apparel.

RIBBED WEAVE

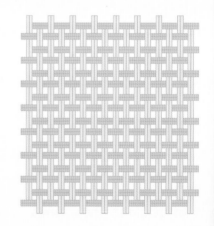

WHAT IT IS: A plain-weave style of fabric, where the weft threads are larger in size than the warp threads.

WHAT IT DOES: Because the weft threads are larger, this creates a "rib," which forms a texture on the surface of the fabric.

WHY USE IT: The ribs can create an interesting texture, especially when the warp and weft threads are different colors.

PIQUÉ

WHAT IT IS: A style of both knit and woven fabrics with a waffle-like structure, also known as marcella.

WHAT IT DOES: The weave is created with a fine ribbing, which helps to hold starch for a crisper, more formal garment.

WHY USE IT: Knit piqué fabric is often used in polo shirts, while woven piqué fabrics are typically used when making suit coats and bow ties in men's formalwear.

KNITS

WHAT THEY ARE: Knit fabrics have threads that are knitted together in a looping method, much like the process of knitting with yarn.

WHAT THEY DO: When threads are knitted together instead of woven, the resulting fabric has a natural stretch, making it suitable for stretch fabric designs.

WHY USE THEM: Most activewear, intimate apparel, and swimsuits use stretch knit fabrics, as they will form around the body but without restraining movement.

HERRINGBONE

WHAT IT IS: A twill-weave style
of fabric, where the fibers form a
V-shaped pattern.

WHAT IT DOES: Herringbone
can be made of a single color or
alternating thread colors; the fish-
like print is unique to this fabric.

WHY USE IT: Often used in
wool suiting and cotton shirting,
a herringbone weave is always a
timeless choice.

 SEE ALSO: Twill, page 105

HOUNDSTOOTH

WHAT IT IS: A twill-weave style
of fabric, where the fibers form a
distinctive check pattern.

WHAT IT DOES: The warp and
weft threads form the check by
weaving two over, then two under,
with one additional thread moving
forward at each check.

WHY USE IT: This traditional
Scottish print has been used for suit
making for generations, and never
goes out of style.

 SEE ALSO: Twill, page 105

ARGYLE

WHAT IT IS: A traditional Scottish design featuring three different-colored threads woven into a print.

WHAT IT DOES: Argyle is formed of stacked diamond shapes, with lines on top creating an X through the center of the diamonds.

WHY USE IT: This fabric is a must for traditional Scottish garments and socks!

JACQUARD

WHAT IT IS: A style of woven fabric that includes brocade and damask, where the print is formed with the threads rather than with ink applied to the surface of the fabric.

WHAT IT DOES: Created by Joseph Marie Jacquard, the loom used to weave jacquard allows the weft threads to move independently, resulting in more design control and more intricate details.

WHY USE IT: Unlike printed designs that will fade with time, jacquard designs are woven, creating a pattern that will last forever.

TAFFETA

WHAT IT IS: A fabric with a plain weave and a crisp drape, typically made from silk or synthetic threads.

WHAT IT DOES: Yarn-dyed taffeta, where the threads are dyed before weaving, is slightly stiffer than piece-dyed taffeta, where the fabric is dyed after the weaving process.

WHY USE IT: For formalwear that requires a fabric to hold its shape, taffeta is a better choice than silks or satins, which are much smoother.

 SEE ALSO: Plain weave, page 104

CHIFFON

WHAT IT IS: A sheer fabric typically made of silk or synthetic fibers twisted together and then woven in a plain weave.

WHAT IT DOES: The transparent fabric has a lovely drape and is often used in dressmaking, in particular for eveningwear.

WHY USE IT: The unique crepe texture created by the twisted fibers creates a luxurious textile that elevates the most basic shape.

CHINO

WHAT IT IS: A fabric with a twill weave, typically woven from medium-weight 100 percent cotton threads, though occasionally made from cotton and synthetic blends.

WHAT IT DOES: The twill weave and natural material provide strength, which makes this fabric ideal for pants, resulting in the "chino" pant.

WHY USE IT: If the fiber is strong enough for soldiers' pants, it's likely strong enough for yours!

FIL-À-FIL/END-ON-END

WHAT IT IS: A fabric made of two different thread colors on the warp and the weft.

WHAT IT DOES: The two colors form a subtle random allover print that reads as depth and texture.

WHY USE IT: Commonly known as chambray, this fabric is often used in dressmaking, shirting, and other fine apparel making.

SATIN

WHAT IT IS: A fabric created by employing a satin weave, which provides a shimmering right side and a matte wrong side; most often made from silk or polyester threads.

WHAT IT DOES: The satin weave, which is produced when four or more warp threads float over the weft threads, or vice versa, creates warp-faced or weft-faced satins.

WHY USE IT: The weave creates a reflective face, resulting in a fabric that is ideal for formalwear, lingerie, blouses, and other fluid garments.

 SEE ALSO: Satin weave, page 106

FLANNEL

WHAT IT IS: A fabric typically made from cotton, wool, or synthetic fibers. It is woven and then brushed with a fine metal comb to provide softness.

WHAT IT DOES: Offers a natural fiber that is extremely soft and breathable, and available in a range of drapes and weights.

WHY USE IT: Wool flannel is often used in suit making; cotton flannel is ideal for children's wear and men's shirts due to its softness.

MOLESKIN

WHAT IT IS: A medium-weight to heavyweight fabric made from cotton that has a soft pile nap on the right side and the weave structure on the wrong side.

WHAT IT DOES: The pile is formed by shaving the face of the fabric after weaving to create the short pile nap, which has a similar feel to velvet.

WHY USE IT: Moleskin is both strong and soft, making it a durable and easy-care alternative to velvet.

 SEE ALSO: Nap, page 121; Pile, page 120

DRILL

WHAT IT IS: A fabric made of natural fibers, featuring a diagonal twill weave.

WHAT IT DOES: The twill weave provides strength and, when used in combination with heavier threads, can be used for making uniforms and sportswear.

WHY USE IT: Drill is another fine choice when requiring a strong and durable fabric made from breathable natural fibers.

CORDUROY

WHAT IT IS: A woven fabric typically made with cotton fibers, with cord ribs (or "wales") that are parallel to each other.

WHAT IT DOES: The pile of the fabric creates a nap, resulting in a smooth fabric in one direction, and a rough one in the opposite, much like velvet, but with ribs.

WHY USE IT: The natural fibers of corduroy create a durable yet soft fabric, ideal for pants, jackets, and shirts, depending on the heaviness of the ribs.

VOILE

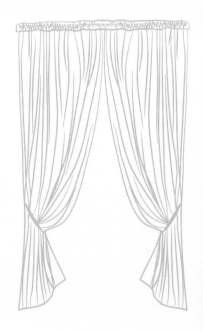

WHAT IT IS: A very lightweight and often sheer fabric made from either cotton or synthetic fibers.

WHAT IT DOES: Provides options for sheerness and layering for home décor or apparel construction.

WHY USE IT: The translucence of voile makes it an ideal choice for drapery, loungewear, and also summer dresses.

LASTEX

WHAT IT IS: An elastic thread that provides stretch in the thread and the finished fabric.

WHAT IT DOES: Made from either a natural or synthetic fiber core wrapped with lastex elastic, when woven into fabric this thread provides a one- or two-way stretch.

WHY USE IT: Lastex is an ideal fiber for activewear, swimwear, and shapewear garments.

TOILE

WHAT IT IS: A traditional cotton fabric that originated in Europe in the eighteenth century. (Also used to refer to a test garment, or "muslin," in the UK.)

WHAT IT DOES: Toile fabric is a white or off-white fabric printed with a pastoral scene in a single color of ink.

WHY USE IT: Classic toile prints have remained popular for many generations. They are mostly used for home décor, but are occasionally also used for garments.

 SEE ALSO: Muslin, page 103

FELT

WHAT IT IS: A non-woven cloth that is commonly made from wool or acrylic.

WHAT IT DOES: Felt is formed by compressing, matting, and pushing the raw materials into shape, unlike other fabrics, which are woven from threads.

WHY USE IT: Often used in crafting, felt can be molded, cut, glued, and sewn. As it doesn't have a weave structure, it won't unravel or fray like typical fabric. However, it is not as strong as fabric, so keep that in mind when considering it.

BAIZE

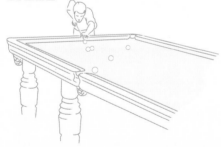

WHAT IT IS: Commonly confused for felt, baize is a woven fabric made from cotton or wool, and typically produced in red or green.

WHAT IT DOES: The surface of the fabric doesn't pill and is stronger than felt since it is woven. It is rather smooth and slick, which is why it is often found on pool tables, gaming tables, corkboards, and dart boards.

WHY USE IT: When you need a fiber similar to felt, but require greater strength and sew-ability, baize is the perfect (and often overlooked) choice.

DOUBLE GAUZE

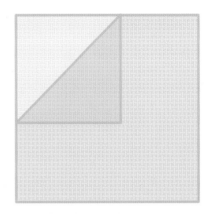

WHAT IT IS: A fabric consisting of two thin layers of cotton gauze that are woven with a leno weave.

WHAT IT DOES: A leno weave creates a strong but lightweight fabric as two warp threads are wrapped around a weft thread. The layers of the gauze are then woven together at intervals to create a double layer.

WHY USE IT: Double gauze is very drapey and soft, making it ideal for décor, as well as all kinds of garments, including children's wear.

AIDA CLOTH

WHAT IT IS: A cotton fabric with a loose, even weave, available in a range of colors.

WHAT IT DOES: Most often used for cross-stitch, the weave of this cloth provides a grid to use when counting and embroidering your design.

WHY USE IT: While you can embroider on nearly any fabric, cross-stitch is largely about counting on a grid, and this cloth helpfully keeps threads evenly spaced.

PRINT

WHAT IT IS: A print is imagery that is screen-printed or stamped on to fabric.

WHAT IT DOES: Unlike woven designs, like jacquard, where the design is formed by the warp and weft threads, a print is placed on the surface of the fabric after the fabric has been woven.

WHY USE IT: Printed fabric offers an incredibly wide range of style choices, so don't limit yourself to just woven designs or you'll miss out on a huge percentage of fabrics.

 SEE ALSO: Jacquard, page 109

MOTIF

WHAT IT IS: The design featured on a fabric; it may be screen-printed, stamped, or woven.

WHAT IT DOES: A motif, whether large or small, is what is used to embellish plain fabric.

WHY USE IT: Plain fabrics have their time and place, but a fabric with motif designs can open the door to many creative options.

REPEAT

WHAT IT IS: The distance between motifs on a piece of fabric.

WHAT IT DOES: Some fabrics feature a single image that is repeated in a variety of grids or diagonals, showing some of the base cloth behind; others are large scenes that repeat without a break in the design itself.

WHY USE IT: The size of a repeat can directly affect the busyness of a fabric—a simple repeated icon will be less bold than a large print.

DIRECTIONAL PRINT

WHAT IT IS: A fabric with a print that has a clear top and bottom.

WHAT IT DOES: A directional print requires that all pieces be cut in the same direction so that the motif remains consistently upright on the finished project.

WHY USE IT: Because super fun prints are often directional! Just remember to purchase additional fabric so that all pattern pieces can be placed in the same direction during the cutting process.

PRINT AND NAP

BORDER PRINT

WHAT IT IS: A fabric with a print that is designed with the selvage edge as a focal point.

WHAT IT DOES: A border print has a print that typically runs crossgrain instead of with the length of grain, often with directional consideration.

WHY USE IT: Using a border print can give garments a custom feel as you can place the print at specific spots, such as hems and necklines.

PILE

WHAT IT IS: The raised fibers above the face of a woven textile.

WHAT IT DOES: The pile is created by an extra set of warp threads that are left standing up on the surface of the fabric. In some types of fabric these loops are left intact; in others they are cut or trimmed.

WHY USE IT: Examples of pile fabrics are faux fur and velvet, both perfect when something specific is required for a special project.

NAP

WHAT IT IS: Nap is the texture left on pile fabrics.

WHAT IT DOES: The pile on fabrics such as velvet or corduroy has a right and wrong direction, as the light reflects in one way or the other. All pieces of a garment require cutting in the same direction or the light will hit the pieces differently, making the nap appear inconsistent.

WHY USE IT: Fabrics with nap can be especially luxurious to wear, and are popular for suiting and fine dressmaking.

 SEE ALSO: With nap, page 138

REMNANT

WHAT IT IS: A leftover piece of fabric from a bolt in a fabric store.

WHAT IT DOES: Fabric stores will often sell their remnants for discounted prices since they are bolt ends.

WHY USE IT: When working on small projects or quilting, remnants can be a very inexpensive way to acquire fabrics.

PRE-CUTS

WHAT THEY ARE: Pre-cut fabric pieces for quilting and small projects.

WHAT THEY DO: Smallest to largest, standard sizes are: mini charm ($2^{1}/_{2}$ x $2^{1}/_{2}$ in/6 x 6 cm); charm (5 x 5 in/13 x 13 cm); jelly roll ($2^{1}/_{2}$ x 44 in/6 x 112 cm); layer cake (10 x 10 in/25.5 x 25.5 cm); fat eighth (9 x 21 in/23 x 53 cm); fat quarter (18 x 21 in/46 x 53 cm).

WHY USE THEM: Perfect for quilting or items where many pieces of the same size are required, using a pre-cut pack can reduce the amount of cutting significantly.

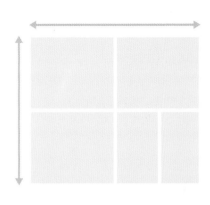

 SEE ALSO: Quilting (stitch), page 88; Quilting (technique), page 186

BLOCK

WHAT IT IS: One of many sections that go together to form a quilt top.

WHAT IT DOES: A block might be a simple single square, or a series of fussy cut pieces that have been sewn together. These blocks are then combined to form the quilt top.

WHY USE IT: Making blocks is the traditional way of building the focal point of a finished quilt. There are thousands of quilt block designs to choose from.

QUILT BACKING

WHAT IT IS: The underside of a finished quilt.

WHAT IT DOES: Unlike the top, pieced side of the quilt, the backing does not provide a focus, so it typically consists largely of a main fabric and some optional accents.

WHY USE IT: To form a quilt, the back is critical, but you can have fun with it and make it as fancy or plain as you like.

 SEE ALSO: Quilting (stitch), page 88; Quilting (technique), page 186

BATTING/WADDING

WHAT IT IS: The fibers that are sandwiched between the quilt top and back, typically made of cotton, polyester, or bamboo.

WHAT IT DOES: The batting provides the loft of the quilt, determining how fluffy or flat the end product will be.

WHY USE IT: You can make a quilt without any batting, which would simply be two layers of fabric quilted together, but the batting provides both the fluff and the warmth.

PRESHRINKING

WHAT IT IS: Preparing your fabric for the cutting and sewing process by washing and drying it.

WHAT IT DOES: This ensures that any shrinking that occurs when the fabric comes in contact with water or heat happens before it is sewn, not after the garment is complete.

WHY USE IT: If the garment you have painstakingly sewn shrinks after being washed, it may then no longer fit you.

MERCERIZATION

WHAT IT IS: Treating fabric and thread made from cotton to add luster and strength.

WHAT IT DOES: Cotton is treated with sodium hydroxide to enlarge the fibers, then soaked in an acid bath to neutralize the fibers. This preshrinks the fabric and provides a smoother surface for a more lustrous finish.

WHY USE IT: If planning on dyeing fabric yourself, make sure the fibers have been mercerized, as they take to dye better than those that have not been treated.

COLORFASTNESS

WHAT IT IS: When fabric is colorfast, this guarantees the inks will retain their original color.

WHAT IT DOES: The inks used in the manufacturing of fabric are treated and washed to ensure that they will not bleed or run in the washing and drying process, or fade when placed in light.

WHY USE IT: Colors might bleed from one fabric to other items in your wash if not colorfast, so if you are unsure, always wash a fabric separately the first few times.

LOOM

WHAT IT IS: A tool available in variety of sizes, from handheld to room-sized, used for weaving fibers into fabric.

WHAT IT DOES: Fibers are stretched on the loom to create the length of the fabric, or the warp. Other fibers are then woven between the warp threads to create the width of the fabric, or the weft.

WHY USE IT: A handheld loom can be used to make small items like potholders and trivets, while large looms are used to create fabric yardage. Creating your own one-of-a-kind fibers is a wonderful way to personalize your projects.

CHAPTER 6
PATTERN & GARMENT TERMS

SEWING PATTERN

WHAT IT IS: The blueprint and instructions for a sewing project.

WHAT IT DOES: The pattern itself is a series of shapes that are cut from paper and then from fabric. The instructions tell you how to put the pieces together.

WHY USE IT: To sew a project, you must either use an existing sewing pattern, or draft your own.

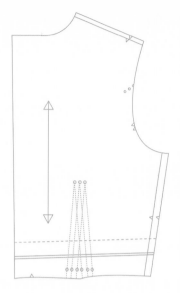

DRAPING

WHAT IT IS: Creating a garment by draping fabric over a body form.

WHAT IT DOES: Pattern drafting is typically done by either draping fabric directly on a form, or by starting flat on paper. Draping demonstrates how a fabric will behave and interact with the body in a three-dimensional way.

WHY USE IT: It can be really helpful for a designer to see how a particular fabric will behave when encountering the curves of the body, as opposed to simply visualizing a finished effect in two dimensions, on flat paper.

DRAFTING

WHAT IT IS: To create sewing pattern pieces on paper.

WHAT IT DOES: When a designer is ready to move from the draping stage to the pattern stage, the shape is transferred from three dimensions to two, and all the markings and seam allowances are added.

WHY USE IT: Drafting pattern pieces allows you to use the same pattern over and over again, and to draft variations on the original shape as well.

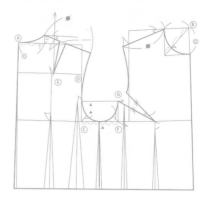

PATTERN PAPER

WHAT IT IS: The tissue paper that a sewing pattern is printed on; the white paper used for pattern drafting; and oaktag paper used in final patternmaking.

WHAT IT DOES: Depending on the stage of the pattern drafting process, there are several different weights of pattern paper that you will encounter.

WHY USE IT: The paper featuring the pattern pieces serves as the plan for an entire project, much like a building's blueprint.

SLOPER

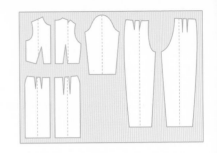

WHAT IT IS: A basic shaped garment sewing pattern, for skirts, tops, pants, and dresses. Also known as a "block."

WHAT IT DOES: A sloper is a base garment that fits you perfectly, which you then use to generate infinite variations.

WHY USE IT: Once you fit a custom sloper to your body, this opens the door to endless creativity! You can take a bodice sloper, for example, then change the neckline to whatever you desire for variations.

ARMSCYE

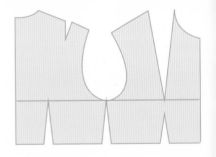

WHAT IT IS: The curve of the pattern from the top of the front shoulder, under the arm, and to the top of the back shoulder.

WHAT IT DOES: It sets the shape of the upper part of the garment, indicating how the piece will fit the body, the arm, and a sleeve, if included.

WHY USE IT: For projects with set-in sleeves, cap sleeves, or even sleeveless garments, the armscye is an important place for proper fit.

GRADING

WHAT IT IS: Enlarging or reducing a pattern piece from its original size to another size.

WHAT IT DOES: Pattern designers make a pattern in one size, then have it graded to additional sizes to suit a wide range of body shapes and sizes.

WHY USE IT: The more sizes a pattern is graded to, the more people can use it!

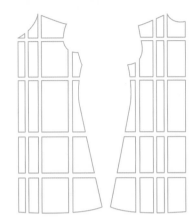

NEST

WHAT IT IS: A series of graded sizes of one pattern piece, all overlapping each other.

WHAT IT DOES: When a pattern piece is nested, the sections where all the sizes are the same end up on top of each other. Where they differ, the lines extend out from one another.

WHY USE IT: The benefit of having all the sizes nested, or overlapping, in this way is that the sewer can then blend from one size to another easily.

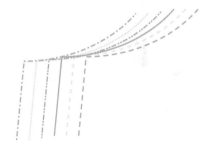

SEAM LINE

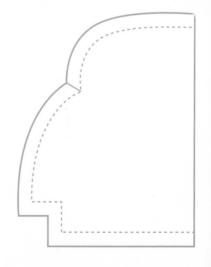

WHAT IT IS: The line inside the cutting line, along which the pieces of a pattern will be sewn together.

WHAT IT DOES: If the seam allowance is included in the pattern, this is the distance between the cutting line and the seam line. Note that the seam line is rarely marked on pattern pieces. Some patterns do not include seam allowance either, in which case the outermost line is the seam line (not the cutting line).

WHY USE IT: Following the indicated seam lines is the only way to get the desired end size and fit based on the original design.

 SEE ALSO: Seam allowance, page 137

CUTTING LINE

WHAT IT IS: The outside line of a pattern piece.

WHAT IT DOES: The cutting lines will be displayed in a variety of styles to differentiate between different sizes. You must follow the line indicating the size you are sewing.

WHY USE IT: If you do not cut along the correct cutting line, you will potentially change the shape of the pattern piece, or accidently make the wrong size.

 SEE ALSO: Nest, page 131; Seam allowance, page 137

BALANCE POINTS

WHAT THEY ARE: Points observed during the patternmaking process that ensure balance in the finished garment.

WHAT THEY DO: Notches and other markings on a pattern are made at key places so the patternmaker can guarantee the garment will hang level from left to right and front to back.

WHY USE THEM: Your item will be off-balance and feel awkward to wear if it is tilting or pulling in any one direction.

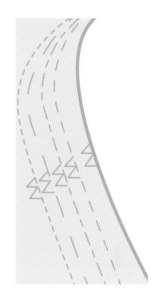

LENGTHEN OR SHORTEN LINE

WHAT IT IS: A line across a pattern piece that is labeled "lengthen or shorten here."

WHAT IT DOES: This tells you the most suitable location for cutting and lengthening or shortening the pattern piece, based on the design of the garment.

WHY USE IT: You would not want to lengthen or shorten a pattern piece through critical construction details, so taking the designer's suggested location is a good idea.

NOTCH

WHAT IT IS: A line or triangle shape along the cutting line on a pattern piece.

WHAT IT DOES: The notches are to be cut or clipped from the fabric to tell you where the pattern pieces should line up during the construction process.

WHY USE IT: Notches are critical indicators that ensure pieces are joining where they should, so this is not something to overlook during the cutting process.

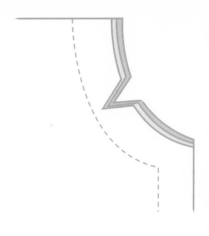

HEMLINE

WHAT IT IS: A line near a skirt, pant, or sleeve hem.

WHAT IT DOES: Projects will have a certain amount of fabric included for a hem, which is the hem allowance, marked by the hem line.

WHY USE IT: The hem amount is calculated to achieve the correct garment length, although it can be altered according to your taste.

DOT

WHAT IT IS: A dot mark on a pattern piece.

WHAT IT DOES: Dots indicate the important construction details on a pattern, like the top and bottom of zippers, the bust apex, gathering marks, and more.

WHY USE IT: All the pattern markings are important for proper construction, dots being no exception to this rule.

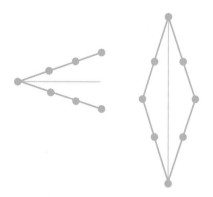

PLACE-ON-FOLD LINE

WHAT IT IS: A line with arrows that point to a certain side of a pattern piece.

WHAT IT DOES: It tells you to place that side of the pattern piece on the fold of the fabric being cut for the project.

WHY USE IT: If the pattern piece was designed to be cut on the fold and you do not do it this way, you will be left with only half of the pattern piece, making it unusable in most cases.

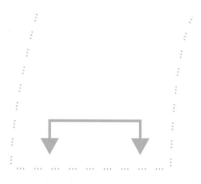

FINISHED GARMENT MEASUREMENTS

WHAT THEY ARE: These summarize the size that a garment will be when sewn according to the pattern's specifications.

WHAT THEY DO: Finished garment measurements tell you how the garment will fit after sewing, which helps when choosing a correct size and understanding the ease of your project.

WHY USE THEM: Each pattern design will have a different amount of ease, so comparing these measurements to the body measurements will help select your correct size.

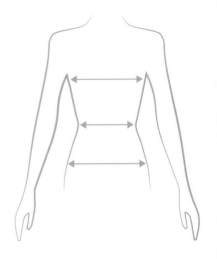

EASE

WHAT IT IS: The distance between the body and the finished garment.

WHAT IT DOES: A fitted woven garment will have 2 in (5 cm) or less ease, whereas a full garment may have 3 in (7.5 cm) or more. Knit garments (which will stretch to fit) can have negative ease, meaning the finished garment is smaller than the body measurements. Ease varies depending on the style of the item and the pattern company's taste.

WHY USE IT: Some items are meant to be fitted and others are meant to be full—understanding the difference will ensure the style is being sewn and worn properly.

CUTTING LAYOUT

WHAT IT IS: The suggested placement of pattern pieces on your fabric for cutting.

WHAT IT DOES: When designers create a sewing pattern, they lay the pattern pieces out on fabric to give the sewer an efficient way to cut the pieces from their fabric, based on the needs of each piece.

WHY USE IT: It is always a good idea to refer to the layout to make sure that pieces that need to be placed on a fold, or cut on the bias, are cut from the fabric correctly.

 SEE ALSO: Bias, page 98

SEAM ALLOWANCE

WHAT IT IS: The distance between the cutting line and the seam line.

WHAT IT DOES: Patterns with included seam allowance will have a certain amount of fabric included around the shape between the line where the piece is cut and the line where the piece is to be sewn. This distance might vary by piece and by company, but a common amount is ⁵⁄₈ in (1.5 cm).

WHY USE IT: If you do not sew at the specified seam allowance, the finished garment will not fit properly, and the pieces will not fit together correctly.

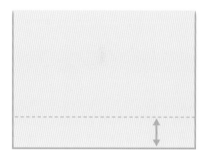

 SEE ALSO: Cutting line, page 132; Seam line, page 132

PATTERN INSTRUCTIONS

WITH NAP

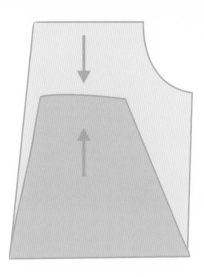

WHAT IT IS: A fabric that has nap.

WHAT IT DOES: Cutting layouts may or may not give a suggested layout for fabrics with nap, ensuring that all the pattern pieces will be head to toe in the same direction.

WHY USE IT: For nap fabrics or directional prints, it's important that all the pieces face the same direction during the cutting process. If the pattern does not indicate the quantity of fabric required for a fabric with nap or direction, you will need to figure out this amount yourself.

 SEE ALSO: Cutting layout, page 137; Directional print, page 119; Nap, page 121

WITHOUT NAP

WHAT IT IS: A fabric that does not have nap.

WHAT IT DOES: Pattern layouts may include layouts for fabrics with or without nap. If your fabric does not have nap or direction, the cutting layout can be reconfigured to maximize the fabric and use less.

WHY USE IT: For allover prints or solid fabrics, the pattern pieces can face either direction.

FULL BUST ADJUSTMENT

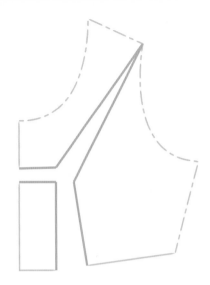

WHAT IT IS: A pattern adjustment for a bust that is larger than the pattern is designed for.

WHAT IT DOES: A full bust adjustment, or FBA as it is commonly called, changes the shape of the pattern piece that includes the bust from a smaller cup size to a larger cup size.

WHY USE IT: If your body fits into one size chart of the pattern but your bust belongs to a much larger size chart, an FBA will change only the bust portion of the pattern, leaving the rest of the pattern to fit at a smaller size.

SMALL BUST ADJUSTMENT

WHAT IT IS: A pattern adjustment for a bust that is smaller than the pattern is designed for.

WHAT IT DOES: A small bust adjustment, or SBA, changes the shape of the pattern piece for the bust from a larger cup size to a smaller cup size.

WHY USE IT: If your body fits into one size chart of the pattern but your bust belongs to a much smaller size chart, a SBA will reduce just the bust area of the pattern, leaving the rest to fit at the larger size.

DART

WHAT IT IS: A triangular fold in the fabric that is stitched in from the edge of a pattern piece to the triangle's point.

WHAT IT DOES: The fabric is folded down the center of the triangle so that the legs of the dart overlap and meet at the point, or apex. The dart is then sewn along the legs, with the stitching ending at the apex.

WHY USE IT: A dart permanently folds fabric to form it around the curves of the body at key spots, such as the bust, upper back, and waist. Darts are therefore necessary for any fitted garment.

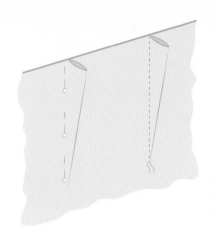

TUCK

WHAT IT IS: A fold in the fabric that is stitched on the right side to keep the fold creased.

WHAT IT DOES: Fabric is folded and stitched a small distance from the fold itself, then repeated over and over at equal distances from each other, forming tucks. The tucks are then pressed flat.

WHY USE IT: Tucks are often used like stitched-down pleats, to reduce volume in one area and open it at another. They are also used for visual detail.

GATHERING

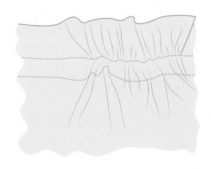

WHAT IT IS: This is used to reduce a larger section of fabric to fit to a smaller section of fabric.

WHAT IT DOES: Gathering fabric is done by sewing two rows of basting stitches, then pulling up on one side of the threads to condense the volume of fabric into a smaller area.

WHY USE IT: Gathering adds fullness to areas for both visual interest and fitting. It is most commonly found at waists, sleeve caps, under the bust, and is used to create ruffles.

ELASTIC SHIRRING

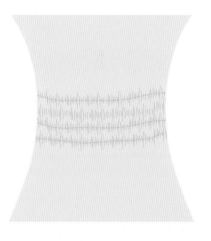

WHAT IT IS: An area on a garment that has been sewn with elastic thread to create stretch.

WHAT IT DOES: To make elastic shirring, elastic thread is hand wound onto the bobbin, then sewn with regular thread. The fabric will shirr and become stretchy. This is made even more stretchy when steamed with an iron.

WHY USE IT: Shirring provides an attractive alternative to elastic in garment construction.

KNIFE PLEAT

WHAT IT IS: Knife pleats form a series of crisply pressed folds in fabric, all going in the same direction.

WHAT IT DOES: Each pleat is three layers of firmly pressed fabric—one on top, one in the middle pointing in the opposite direction, and one behind the pleat.

WHY USE IT: Knife pleats are often found on skirts and dresses to add volume without the poof of gathering.

BOX PLEAT

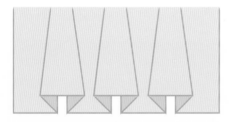

WHAT IT IS: A small section of firmly pressed fabric with two folds behind it, facing each other at the center point of the front fabric.

WHAT IT DOES: Two knife pleats, face to face, sit underneath a third section of fabric, that is equal to the distance of the pleat width.

WHY USE IT: The front "boxes" create a flat surface than opens to expose the underside when worn.

INVERTED PLEAT

WHAT IT IS: The inverse of a box pleat, with two folds facing a center point, and an equal width of fabric behind the two front folds forming the "box."

WHAT IT DOES: The two pleats on top are essentially two knife pleats, face to face, with the third layer of fabric spanning the entire width of the two on top. All are pressed crisp.

WHY USE IT: The underlayer of fabric opens while wearing a skirt or dress with inverted pleats, revealing the volume.

STITCHED-DOWN PLEAT

WHAT IT IS: A pleat that is sewn down part of its length.

WHAT IT DOES: The stitching controls the volume of the pleats until the stitching ends, allowing the fullness of the folds to open at that point.

WHY USE IT: To control the location where the volume is released. Stitched-down pleats are commonly used on skirts, dresses, and pants.

LAPPED ZIPPER

WHAT IT IS: A style of zipper where a thin piece of fabric the same length and width of the zipper itself hides the zipper as part of a seam.

WHAT IT DOES: When inserting a lapped zipper into the seam of a garment, an extra fold of fabric is made so it "laps" over the zipper teeth and keeps it from being visible.

WHY USE IT: Found often on dresses, skirts, and pants with side-seam zippers, this is an elegant way to hide an otherwise utilitarian closure.

FLY-FRONT ZIPPER

WHAT IT IS: A style of zipper opening with a U-shaped flap covering the zipper and topped with a button.

WHAT IT DOES: Typically found on jeans and pants, a zipper is sewn into the sides of the crotch opening with an extra flap of fabric that completely conceals the whole zipper.

WHY USE IT: For a traditional look on pants, a fly-front zipper is the most obvious choice.

BOUND BUTTONHOLE

WHAT IT IS: A style of buttonhole where two pieces of fabric are folded on the wrong side and meet in the center of the hole.

WHAT IT DOES: An extra piece of fabric is sewn to the main piece and cut to create an opening. This extra piece is then folded so that two folds appear in the center of the opening. The end result is an opening that is entirely made of fabric, with no exterior stitching.

WHY USE IT: A bound buttonhole is a gorgeous detail on jackets and more formal garments, as no topstitching or machine buttonholes are visible from the outside of the garment.

PLACKET

WHAT IT IS: A spot in a garment where an opening is located and closures are sewn.

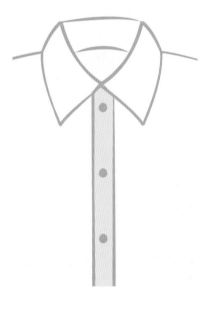

WHAT IT DOES: Found down the front of a dress shirt or on skirts and pants, a placket is most often formed from multiple layers of fabric and interfacing. They have closures sewn into them, like buttons and buttonholes. Sometimes a placket is purely decorative, but most often they are functional.

WHY USE IT: A placket provides stability for the opening and closing of a garment, as well as for the sewing of buttonholes and buttons.

IN-SEAM POCKET

WHAT IT IS: A style of pocket that is sewn into an existing seam.

WHAT IT DOES: One half of a pocket is sewn to one side of the seam and the other half of a pocket is sewn to the other side. These two halves are then joined and the pocket is formed in the process. Its opening is in line with the finished side seam.

WHY USE IT: Because everything is better with a pocket!

WELT POCKET

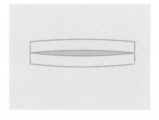

WHAT IT IS: A style of pocket where the pocket is hidden on the inside of the garment and no topstitching is visible on the right side.

WHAT IT DOES: A slit is made in the garment where the opening is to be, then the pocket is sewn to the inside. The opening is finished much like a bound buttonhole, whereby the opening is completed with a piece of fabric that is folded and all the stitching is hidden on the inside.

WHY USE IT: If you desire the functionality of a patch pocket but want something more formal, a welt pocket is a perfect choice.

 SEE ALSO: Bound buttonhole, page 145

PATCH POCKET

WHAT IT IS: A style of pocket that is sewn to the exterior of a garment.

WHAT IT DOES: Cut any shape and size you like, then sew it to a project with an opening at the top and you have a patch pocket.

WHY USE IT: Found on shirts as chest pockets, on the rear of pants, or on the fronts of skirts and dresses for your hands, these are very functional yet fun additions to any garment.

BREAK

WHAT IT IS: The point in the front of pants where the garment folds in on itself.

WHAT IT DOES: Pants can be customized to have a variety of "breaks," depending on the formality or casualness of the style. It all depends on the amount left on the hem, and where it hits the wearer's shoes.

WHY USE IT: To tailor your pants to the occasion, taking the break into account will set a tone for the outfit.

BODICE

WHAT IT IS: The upper portion of a dress, from the waist to the neck.

WHAT IT DOES: A bodice forms the top half of a dress and it includes the armscye, bust, sleeves, and neckline.

WHY USE IT: The bodice portion of a dress can be shaped and fitted a million ways, so consider it a blank canvas for personal style.

 SEE ALSO: Armscye, page 130

FACING

WHAT IT IS: A piece of fabric that is sewn to the outer edges of a garment, finishing them at the same time.

WHAT IT DOES: If a garment doesn't have a lining, it likely has facings, which are shortened versions of the outer layers, sewn to the edges and flipped to the inside where they remain hidden.

WHY USE IT: Less bulky than a full lining, facings are easy ways to achieve clean finishing on the edges.

 SEE ALSO: Understitch, page 82

COWL

WHAT IT IS: A draped neckline style of varying depth and fullness.

WHAT IT DOES: A cowl neckline hangs in loose folds around the neck of a garment.

WHY USE IT: Most commonly this style of neckline is found on the front of a top or dress, but in vintage styles, a cowl can also appear down the back of a garment for dramatic impact.

FALL

WHAT IT IS: A term used to describe the way fabric cascades.

WHAT IT DOES: It can be used to describe the drape of a fabric itself, or the cut of a garment and the way the style "falls" down the body.

WHY USE IT: Because sometimes it provides the perfect description of your beautiful new garment!

FULLNESS

WHAT IT IS: A term to describe an abundance of volume in a garment.

WHAT IT DOES: Fullness is created by gathering, pleating, and shirring, and in any areas of a garment where extra fabric collects to create volume.

WHY USE IT: Using fullness to shape a garment as well as hide areas of the body is what garment construction is all about!

 SEE ALSO: Elastic shirring, page 141; Gathering, page 141

FLOUNCE

WHAT IT IS: An extra bit of fabric that is used as decorative detail.

WHAT IT DOES: Whether it is small and gathered, or larger and cut on a curve to create a ruffle, a flounce can be found on any garment in any spot, but is always entirely decorative.

WHY USE IT: Because sometimes you need a bit of decorative flounce!

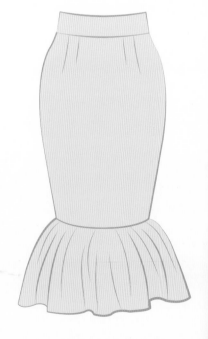

GODET

WHAT IT IS: A triangular-shaped piece of fabric that is sewn into an opening between two seams.

WHAT IT DOES: Godet panels are sewn into openings to create fullness and volume. The flare of the fabric also gives the garment extra movement.

WHY USE IT: Typically used in skirt and dress hems, a godet is a feminine detail that can add a lot of flow to an otherwise stiff garment.

FLARE

WHAT IT IS: A term used to describe fullness in a garment.

WHAT IT DOES: A "fit and flare" dress is one that has a fitted upper half (bodice) and fully flared bottom half (skirt). The flare might be achieved with an A-line, gathered, gored, or pleated skirt, as all will provide fullness.

WHY USE IT: When discussing garment details, flare can be a good all-purpose term—it gets your point across without having to specify how the flare is formed.

SCALLOP

WHAT IT IS: A half-circle curve in the fabric that meets with another scallop at the half-circle mark.

WHAT IT DOES: Simply sewing along the half-circle shape, then repeating, will create scallops along the edge of any seam.

WHY USE IT: Scallops can be found on the hem of pants, shorts, skirts, dresses, and along detailed seams like jacket fronts and collars. It adds an element of whimsy and fun to any item.

EMPIRE WAIST

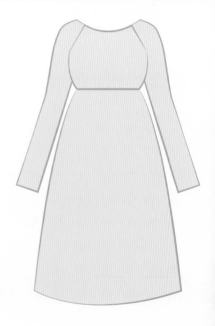

WHAT IT IS: A garment that has a seam just under the bust, with the rest of the volume falling from that point.

WHAT IT DOES: The empire waist creates a faux high waist and can be used for tops, jackets, and dresses.

WHY USE IT: Especially great if you want to hide the mid-section of the body. This shape has all the fullness starting under the bust, hiding the rest of the body under its layers.

CASING

WHAT IT IS: A channel inside a garment which is intended to have something fed through it, such as a drawstring or elastic.

WHAT IT DOES: Used most often at waists, a casing provides shaping by fitting a garment to the body with the addition of drawstring or elastic.

WHY USE IT: Perfect for use on elastic-waisted skirts, pajama pants, or dresses with a drawstring waist tie, a casing provides an easy approach to garment construction.

GUSSET

WHAT IT IS: An inset piece of fabric that is sewn into the underarm area of a garment.

WHAT IT DOES: This square- or triangular-shaped piece provides movement in a fitted garment.

WHY USE IT: If you require a free range of motion in the arms when making a garment with a fitted bodice, a gusset can be very helpful.

PRINCESS SEAM

WHAT IT IS: A curved seam that runs from the upper part of the bodice, down the bust or back, and then ends at the waist seam or hem of the garment.

WHAT IT DOES: Provides shaping and fitting without the use of darts.

WHY USE IT: Mostly this is a style preference, but a princess seam can be an easier way to adjust fit for a full bust as the seam curves over the bust instead of pointing at it.

PEPLUM

WHAT IT IS: An overskirt that is sewn onto the hem of a top or jacket, which is then worn over the top of another garment.

WHAT IT DOES: Like a small miniskirt, a peplum is typically cut like a circle skirt to create a ruffle around the hip.

WHY USE IT: A peplum can add a lot of vintage flair, as well as hide a fuller hip.

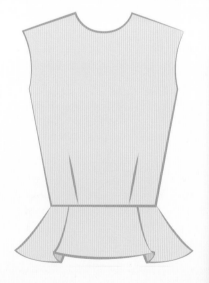

FRENCH DART

WHAT IT IS: A long dart that starts at the side seam, typically at or below the waist, and then curves up to the bust apex.

WHAT IT DOES: This type of dart eliminates bulky fabric through the middle of a dress, while providing subtle shaping.

WHY USE IT: Found often in shift dresses, a French dart is an understated way to achieve shaping, whereas traditional bust darts tend to be more tailored and fitted.

SLEEVE HEAD

WHAT IT IS: The uppermost top corner of the sleeve at the shoulder.

WHAT IT DOES: This area is where the garment will reveal fit and construction issues, as the sleeve head might collapse if too big or unsupported from within.

WHY USE IT: On tailored jackets and blazers, the sleeve head must fit properly and be interlined or it will appear too large, or fold and crease under the seam.

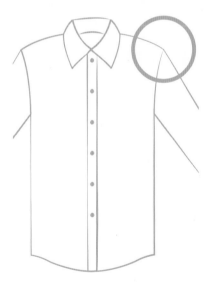

SET-IN SLEEVE

WHAT IT IS: A style of sleeve where the top of the sleeve is sewn into the circle of the armscye without puckers or gathers in the seam.

WHAT IT DOES: Both the side seam of the garment and the side seam of the sleeve are sewn first, then the sleeve is eased into the armscye to fit, with a smooth seam.

WHY USE IT: This is a classic fitted sleeve, found on tops, jackets, dresses, and more. It can be tricky to ease in without any puckers, and is one of the hardest sleeves to sew.

 SEE ALSO: Armscye, page 130

CAP SLEEVE

WHAT IT IS: A type of short sleeve that only extends from the upper part of the armscye.

WHAT IT DOES: A cap sleeve is sewn to the top of the armscye and then tapers to nothing as it approaches the side seam of the garment. The sleeve does not reach the side seam, and that portion of the garment is finished in another way—with a facing or bias tape.

WHY USE IT: A cap sleeve achieves a very similar look to a set-in sleeve but is much easier to sew.

 SEE ALSO: Facing, page 148; Bias tape, page 47

RAGLAN SLEEVE

WHAT IT IS: A type of sleeve with a diagonal seam from the collarbone to under the arm on the front, and the neck to underarm on the back.

WHAT IT DOES: This is the easiest sleeve to sew, since there is no curved armscye to set a sleeve into. Rather, the sleeve seams are sewn along the front and back of the garment, much like a straight seam.

WHY USE IT: Apart from being easy, this sleeve creates an interesting design detail; the diagonal seaming can also be finished with topstitching.

 SEE ALSO: Armscye, page 130

DOLMAN SLEEVE

WHAT IT IS: A type of sleeve that is formed from the front and back pieces of the garment itself.

WHAT IT DOES: Most often there is a seam from the neck, over the shoulder, and down the arm to the hem, as this is where the front and backs are joined, forming the sleeve at the same time.

WHY USE IT: A dolman sleeve creates a draped-style sleeve, perfect for use with lightweight fabrics such as silk, rayon, or knits.

BISHOP SLEEVE

WHAT IT IS: A type of sleeve with a very full arm and a gathered hem, most often into a sleeve cuff.

WHAT IT DOES: The fullest sleeve to wear, a bishop sleeve is a very formal sleeve, typically found on eveningwear and gowns.

WHY USE IT: If you are looking for drama in a sleeve, the bishop sleeve is the right choice!

FLAT COLLAR

WHAT IT IS: A style of collar that is sewn completely flat to the neckline.

WHAT IT DOES: A flat collar provides visual interest and, because it is flat, it is extremely easy to sew. It can be sewn to any type of garment and it does not require that the garment have an opening with a button and placket.

WHY USE IT: Flat collars can be nearly any shape or size. Since you are not limited to the construction of the garment either, adding them can be easy and fun.

COLLAR POINT

WHAT IT IS: The farthest end point of a collar.

WHAT IT DOES: A collar point can be shaped in a wide range of angles, and its sharpness will determine its level of formality.

WHY USE IT: Most men's dress shirts have a pointed collar and these can be reshaped to the wearer's desired angle.

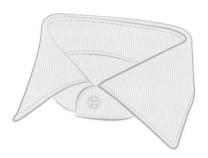

COLLAR STAND

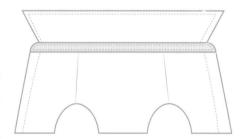

WHAT IT IS: A small band of fabric that connects a collar to the rest of the garment.

WHAT IT DOES: Found on men's dress shirts, a collar stand is a traditional approach for shirt making, where the stand is sewn to the shirt and then the collar is sewn into the stand and pressed crisp.

WHY USE IT: A collar stand is a must for classic tailoring and for giving the collar height around the neck.

PETER PAN COLLAR

WHAT IT IS: A collar shape with dramatically rounded curves that meet at the center front.

WHAT IT DOES: Found most often on flat collars, and named for the fictional character Peter Pan, this style of collar adds whimsy to any garment.

WHY USE IT: For instant charm, nothing does it faster than a Peter Pan collar!

ROLLED COLLAR

WHAT IT IS: A style of collar that rolls out from the neck, overlapping the seam where it was attached.

WHAT IT DOES: Unlike a collar that has a crisp, pressed edge, a rolled collar is attached to the garment directly, or attached to a collar stand, then folded over the seam toward the body.

WHY USE IT: A rolled collar is a great choice for a softer collar, or for projects with thick fabrics that cannot form a pressed edge, such as a woolen jacket.

POINTED COLLAR

WHAT IT IS: A collar shape with points that meet at the center front.

WHAT IT DOES: A more formal approach to a collar, a pointed collar is found on everything from men's dress shirts to children's wear, and can be made in either the style of a flat collar or a rolled collar.

WHY USE IT: This is a very prim and proper collar, and it can elevate even a simple T-shirt.

ROUNDED COLLAR

WHAT IT IS: A collar featuring slight curves that meet at the center front of the garment.

WHAT IT DOES: Much like a pointed collar, a rounded collar is often found on dress shirts with a collar stand. Compared to a Peter Pan collar, the curve here is much more subtle.

WHY USE IT: When used on a men's dress shirt, a rounded collar can give a slightly softer touch than a traditional pointed collar.

SHIFT

WHAT IT IS: A dress shape that usually hangs a few inches away from the body, has no waist definition, and ends above the knee.

WHAT IT DOES: A timeless shape, a shift dress can be found with many variations, but the basic shape, originating in the 1920s, is always the same.

WHY USE IT: The same reason it gained popularity in the first place: it's comfortable!

TUNIC

WHAT IT IS: A long top that is intended as a layering item and not to be worn independently.

WHAT IT DOES: Whether considered a long top or a short dress, the tunic is always a loose garment, typically worn over pants or leggings.

WHY USE IT: Worn by both men and women since ancient times, the tunic is a timeless means of layering.

PENCIL SKIRT

WHAT IT IS: A form-fitted skirt shape that typically hits at the knee.

WHAT IT DOES: A pencil skirt can be an independent item as well as the lower half of a dress. It sometimes has a slit up the side, center front, or center back to allow for movement.

WHY USE IT: Pencil skirts are inherently full of attitude, so if you are after a saucy shape, this is a classic one to pick.

A-LINE

WHAT IT IS: A shape of a skirt or dress that has a silhouette like a capital letter A.

WHAT IT DOES: The waist of the skirt or dress is like the top of the A, with the legs of the letter forming the path to the hem.

WHY USE IT: The A-line shape is universally flattering as the skirt shape is fitted at the waist—often the smallest part of the body—while the flare glides over the hip.

CHAPTER 7
TECHNIQUES
& PROCESSES

LINING

WHAT IT IS: A second layer of fabric attached to the inside of a finished garment.

WHAT IT DOES: A lining is formed like an entire second garment and is inserted inside the outer garment during the construction process.

WHY USE IT: To provide smoothness or opacity when sewing with clingy or sheer fabrics, or to protect the skin from itchy fabrics like woolens.

UNDERLINING

WHAT IT IS: A layer of lining that is cut to match each fabric pattern piece. Each underlining and corresponding fabric piece is then then joined together and sewn as one unit throughout the construction process.

WHAT IT DOES: Provides strength or opacity to the outer fabric as all the seam elements, darts, and construction details are sewn through both layers.

WHY USE IT: Perfect for see-through fabrics like lace or eyelet, underlining is easy to use as you sew all the garment details as if there is only one piece of fabric.

INTERLINING

WHAT IT IS: Layers of fabric that are inserted into the garment between the main fabric and the lining fabric during construction.

WHAT IT DOES: Interlining provides stability, strength, or warmth to the garment it is sewn to— on the lapel of a blazer, for example.

WHY USE IT: If an item requires more structure than the fabric can provide, then interlining will add extra support.

BAGGED LINING

WHAT IT IS: A lining process that allows for some volume on the inside for movement.

WHAT IT DOES: The process of "bagging" a garment is most often used on jackets and outerwear, where the lining is sewn to the jacket, and then turned right side out through a hole left in the lining, before being closed up afterward.

WHY USE IT: For a lining with minimal to no hand sewing, this is a popular method as it is very easy to do.

SEAMS

BIAS SEAM

WHAT IT IS: A seam where two fabrics meet that is cut on a true 45-degree bias of the fabric.

WHAT IT DOES: Creates a seam that is sewn on a diagonal across the fabric, creating a stretch and flow that is different than a seam sewn on the lengthwise grain or crossgrain of the fabric.

WHY USE IT: When two pieces are being joined, a diagonal seam can reduce bulk as the seam is not in a straight line. Bias seams can also be used for visual interest.

FRENCH SEAM

WHAT IT IS: A seam that looks like a regular seam on the outside, but is enclosed on the inside, leaving only a small flap of fabric.

WHAT IT DOES: Instead of sewing fabric together with right sides facing, you sew with wrong sides facing, then trim down the seam allowance, flip right sides together, and re-sew the seam, creating a small fold of fabric on the inside with all the stitching hidden inside it.

WHY USE IT: Ideal for semi-sheer fabrics where the construction stitches would be visible if sewn with a traditional seam.

FLAT-FELLED SEAM

WHAT IT IS: A seam with two rows of stitching on the right side and a clean seam on the inside.

WHAT IT DOES: A flat-felled seam is finished on the right side of the garment, leaving a clean finish on the wrong side of the fabric, and a folded piece on the right side that has been sewn down on either side to produce two rows of stitching.

WHY USE IT: Commonly used on men's shirts, this is a lovely seam to use as all is hidden, and yet the two rows stitched on the right side create a more casual appearance.

SELF-BOUND SEAM

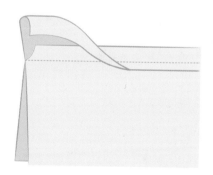

WHAT IT IS: A seam that looks like a regular seam on the right side and has a small fold of fabric on the wrong side, with no exposed stitching.

WHAT IT DOES: Very much like a French seam, this seam has a flap of fabric on the inside hiding the raw edges of the fabric. The difference is that this flap is folded after the seam is sewn and is created by simply folding the seam allowance on itself to self-bind the seam.

WHY USE IT: For a clean and beautiful finish, this is a nice way to mimic a French seam on semi-sheer fabrics or unlined garments.

HONG KONG FINISH

WHAT IT IS: A seam that looks like a regular seam on the right side, and has binding on the raw edges of the fabric on the inside.

WHAT IT DOES: The binding encases the raw edges of the fabric on the inside, thereby keeping the fabric from fraying and creating a clean finish.

WHY USE IT: Perfect for unlined jackets, the binding will finish off thick fabrics that cannot be finished in another clean way.

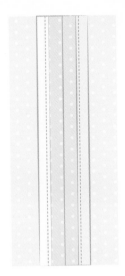

PINKING

WHAT IT IS: Finishing the raw edge of fabric by cutting it with pinking shears.

WHAT IT DOES: Fabric cut with pinking shears will not unravel and weaken the seam.

WHY USE IT: If you are making something casual and want a quick and easy way to finish the seams, simply cutting the fabric with pinking shears is a great solution.

 SEE ALSO: Pinking Shears, page 13

CLIPPING CURVES

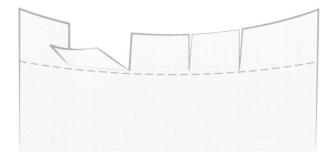

WHAT IT IS: Small slits cut into the seam allowance on concave curves.

WHAT IT DOES: The cuts in the fabric allow the seam allowance to lay flat as the distance between the slits will open and stretch to allow the seam to properly curve.

WHY USE IT: When sewing with curves, clipping or notching is always required to allow the inner or outer curve to behave properly.

NOTCHING CURVES

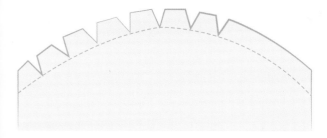

WHAT IT IS: Small V sections of fabric that are cut into the seam allowance on convex curves.

WHAT IT DOES: The sections of fabric that are cut out allow the seam allowance to lay flat as the distance between the Vs will close together without overlapping.

WHY USE IT: When sewing with curves, clipping or notching is always required to allow the inner or outer curve to behave properly.

GRADING SEAMS

WHAT IT IS: A method of trimming the seam allowances on the inside of a garment.

WHAT IT DOES: Each layer of the seam allowance is trimmed to slightly longer or shorter than the preceding layer.

WHY USE IT: To reduce bulk on seams with more than one fabric intersecting so the seam will lay flat.

MITER

WHAT IT IS: The point on a garment where the binding or hem is joined at a corner along a diagonal line.

WHAT IT DOES: As there is less overlapping of fabric, a mitered corner is less bulky and much more professional looking.

WHY USE IT: A mitered corner is not hard to sew, and it makes a lovely finish on items that have two hems meeting at a corner.

PIVOT

WHAT IT IS: A turn in the stitching at a corner or on any other sharp curve.

WHAT IT DOES: When sewing anything with a corner, it is easy to pivot by simply sinking your needle into the fabric, picking up your presser foot, rotating the fabric, lowering the foot, and then continuing with your sewing.

WHY USE IT: A perfectly pivoted corner is a must when edgestitching or topstitching the outer elements of garments.

FINGER PRESS

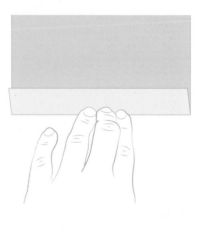

WHAT IT IS: Pressing and molding a seam in place with your fingers.

WHAT IT DOES: Finger pressing can help get things into place prior to pressing with the hot iron.

WHY USE IT: You have much more finesse with your fingers than you do with an iron, and getting things in place with your fingers before ironing can result in a much better pressed seam.

EMBELLISHING

WHAT IT IS: Any decoration added to a plain item.

WHAT IT DOES: Adding embroidery, beads, cording, or any other kind of adornment constitutes embellishment.

WHY USE IT: To add beautification to an otherwise plain purse, dress, skirt, or any other item—embellishment can provide personalization and customization.

CORDING

WHAT IT IS: A decorative fabric-covered cord that is sewn onto the right side of a project.

WHAT IT DOES: Sewn by hand into patterns or designs, cording is purely a decorative embellishment.

WHY USE IT: It looks beautiful when used around a neckline or hem for ornamental decoration.

ROULEAU

WHAT IT IS: A piece of thin fabric formed into a long tube that is sewn onto the right side of a project.

WHAT IT DOES: Sewn by hand into patterns or designs, roleau is much like cording and used for decorative embellishment.

WHY USE IT: Unlike cording, which has thickness to it, rouleau is flat and can be used in slightly different shapes as a result.

APPLIQUÉ

WHAT IT IS: Sewing a patch of fabric onto another larger piece of fabric for decorative purposes.

WHAT IT DOES: The smaller pieces of fabric can be cut into geometric shapes or into elaborate scenes. They are then stitched by hand or machine to pillows, garments, or other sewn projects.

WHY USE IT: As you can cut any shape you like to be appliquéd, there is no limit to the creativity of this technique!

CUTWORK

WHAT IT IS: A style of needlework where a design is embellished with thread, then elements are cut from the fabric to create an open design.

WHAT IT DOES: Used in garments and other sewn projects, the cut holes are filled with embroidery floss or lace thread.

WHY USE IT: Cutwork designs can be found as fabric or as appliqué patches, and can be used to embellish nearly any project.

TATTING

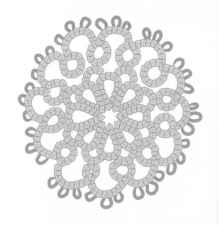

WHAT IT IS: A decorative lace-like trim that is used for making collars and doilies.

WHAT IT DOES: Tatting designs are formed by a series of knots and loops, formed with a medium-weight thread and either a shuttle and hook, or knitting-like needles.

WHY USE IT: This beautiful trim has a long history of use in garment embellishment and home décor because it is elegant and timeless.

BRODERIE ANGLAISE

WHAT IT IS: A style of needlework that features cutwork, embroidery, and lace on fabric, traditionally white in color.

WHAT IT DOES: This is a very old technique for creating decorative shapes in fabric using eyelets that are each bound with thread.

WHY USE IT: This technique has been used since the sixteenth century to create beautiful garments and other sewn projects.

EYELET

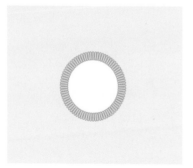

WHAT IT IS: A small hole that has short and closely sewn stitches emanating from the center, usually sewn by hand.

WHAT IT DOES: Provides decorative visual interest in a fabric.

WHY USE IT: To punctuate embellishment or decorate stitching. A hand-sewn eyelet can turn regular fabric into something closer to eyelet fabric.

EMBROIDERY

WHAT IT IS: Hand stitching designs on fabric with embroidery floss and a hand-sewing needle.

WHAT IT DOES: Embroidery is essentially like drawing on fabric with thick thread. There are hundreds of stitches that can be sewn to create two-dimensional images of any kind.

WHY USE IT: Embroidery can be used for home décor, or as embellishment on garments— around hems and necklines, or on yokes.

SASHIKO

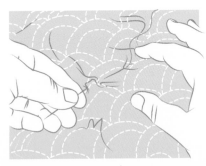

WHAT IT IS: Sashiko is a Japanese style of needlework with small embroidery stitches.

WHAT IT DOES: Small running stitches are traditionally formed with white thread on indigo-dyed cotton fabric for both decoration and reinforcement.

WHY USE IT: For a minimalist approach to embroidery, sashiko stitching is very modern, despite its ancient roots.

KLOSTER BLOCK

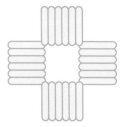

WHAT IT IS: A block of satin stitching, made with five threads stitched closely and at a regular distance to form a perfect square.

WHAT IT DOES: Used entirely for decorative purposes, this counted-thread form of stitching can embellish any item in your closet or home.

WHY USE IT: Revive old stitching techniques by learning to make elaborate designs with very simple stitches.

HUCK WEAVING

WHAT IT IS: A series of stitches forming an ornamental pattern for decorative hand stitching, also known as Swedish weaving or huck embroidery.

WHAT IT DOES: This provides decorative detailing on any garment, and is most commonly found on necklines, yokes, and hems.

WHY USE IT: For the joy of stitching—huck weaving elevates even the simplest tea towel into a family heirloom.

CREWEL

WHAT IT IS: A style of needlework very similar to embroidery where threads are stitched onto fabric following a design.

WHAT IT DOES: Entirely decorative, designs are made using crewel wool and crewel hand-sewing needles, forming elaborate patterns using an embroidery style of stitching.

WHY USE IT: Used for creating decorative art, crewel needlework can be used to make beautiful wall hangings and many other home décor items.

ASSISI

WHAT IT IS: A form of needlework that uses a counted-thread method of stitching.

WHAT IT DOES: Stitching is formed on a grid so that each stitch is counted by the number of grids used. The background of the fabric is filled in with stitches, but the motifs are only outlined following the grid.

WHY USE IT: Named after the Italian town of Assisi, this is an ancient tradition for creating decorative décor.

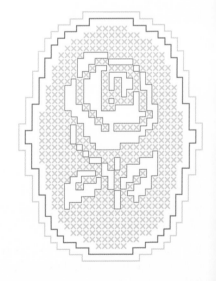

STUMPWORK

WHAT IT IS: Also known as raised embroidery, this is a form of embroidery where some of the shapes are flat and some are raised off the fabric.

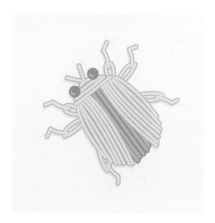

WHAT IT DOES: This embellishment is used for dramatic effect. Wires, filler, and padding are added to the embroidery thread to create three-dimensional designs.

WHY USE IT: Used mostly in home décor, wall hangings come alive when taken from regular embroidery to stumpwork.

SMOCKING

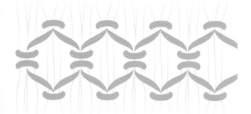

WHAT IT IS: Gathering fabric into sections, usually in a grid or pattern, by hand with needle and thread.

WHAT IT DOES: Reduces the fullness of a garment without elastic in a decorative manner.

WHY USE IT: Smocking can be used as embellishment around detailed spots on a garment, like the neckline or yoke, and it can provide an alternative to gathering or pleats.

BARGELLO

WHAT IT IS: A style of needlework with long stitches formed into graphic shapes of various colors.

WHAT IT DOES: Bargello embroidery work is created with elaborately shaded multicolored patterns that are mapped out with mathematical motifs and usually sewn into wool.

WHY USE IT: This style of patternmaking is complex and beautiful, and can result in beautiful home décor when used on pillows and wall hangings.

GOLDWORK

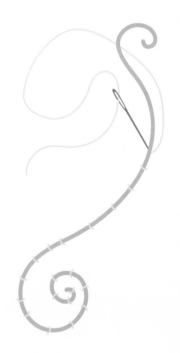

WHAT IT IS: A style of needlework that uses metal threads.

WHAT IT DOES: Gold, silver, and copper threads are stitched to fabric to form elaborate decorative designs on garments and home décor.

WHY USE IT: If you love embroidery but want it to shine, goldwork is the perfect answer!

BLACKWORK

WHAT IT IS: A distinctive style of needlework that uses black thread on white fabric.

WHAT IT DOES: Stitches are formed using both the counted-thread and free-embroidery methods, and they are used for decoration on traditional garments or home décor.

WHY USE IT: Because the black thread on white fabric can look wonderfully modern.

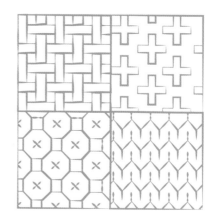

WHITEWORK

WHAT IT IS: A style of needlework that uses white thread on white fabric, usually cotton or linen.

WHAT IT DOES: Whitework can be broderie anglaise, cutwork, or other forms of needlework that involve white as the primary color of thread and background.

WHY USE IT: It provides another form of traditional needlework that can be applied to your garments and home décor projects.

 SEE ALSO: Broderie anglaise, page 177

BEADWORK

WHAT IT IS: Embellishing an item with decorative beads.

WHAT IT DOES: Beads can be used for simple details, or sewn to a garment to form elaborate patterns and designs.

WHY USE IT: Nothing adds flair to a garment faster than sewing beads to it!

SHIBORI

WHAT IT IS: A traditional Japanese method of tying and dyeing fabric to create patterns.

WHAT IT DOES: Most shibori designs are formed by tying, folding, and twisting fabric so as to form circular patterns.

WHY USE IT: Both abstract and patterned designs can be formed by this simple tie-and-dye process.

RESIST

WHAT IT IS: A material applied to fabric that will deliberately repel water or dye.

WHAT IT DOES: Using wax or a similar resist, you can create batik designs or other multilayered prints. Simply paint or stamp the wax onto the fabric and, when dyed, the area that was waxed previously will resist anything liquid.

WHY USE IT: Experiment with multiple stages of dyeing and resist to create some custom fabric for your next project.

PATCHWORK

WHAT IT IS: Sewing small pieces of fabric together to form a larger piece of fabric.

WHAT IT DOES: Creating patchwork is essentially like creating new fabric. The designs may be simple squares or intricate scenes, and can be used in everything from wall hangings to clothing.

WHY USE IT: Another form of expression involving cutting and re-sewing fabric in new and unique ways, this can be a really fun and relaxing hobby.

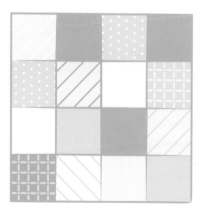

QUILTING

WHAT IT IS: The act of quilting involves stitching through two layers of fabric, plus an in-between filler such as batting.

WHAT IT DOES: Traditionally sewn by hand, but now more often sewn by machine, quilting secures the quilt top to the quilt back, and sandwiches the batting in the middle of the two.

WHY USE IT: The layers of a quilt will not hold in place as well if unsewn, so this is a critical part of quilt making.

 SEE ALSO: Pre-cuts, page 122; Quilting, page 88; Quilting pins, page 25

BINDING

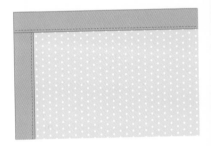

WHAT IT IS: A strip of fabric that is sewn to the edge of a project, like a quilt, that finishes off the raw edges.

WHAT IT DOES: Cut on the bias or on the straight of grain, binding is wrapped around the raw edges and sewn to the project around its perimeter. Used for quilts, blankets, and other similar projects.

WHY USE IT: Binding provides an elegant way to finish off the border of any project.

SQUARING OFF

WHAT IT IS: This involves cutting a clean, straight edge on a project using a ruler and a rotary cutter.

WHAT IT DOES: Often done prior to binding a quilt, but after the quilt stitching, squaring off is a way to ensure true 90-degree corners, and to trim off any excess backing and batting under the quilt top.

WHY USE IT: The process of binding the quilt will go much more smoothly, and your finished quilt look much nicer, if all the edges have been cut straight and are lined up.

BEARDING

WHAT IT IS: Bearding occurs when some of the batting from inside a quilt comes out of the needle holes while quilting.

WHAT IT DOES: The fuzz of batting can pull and be forced out of the needle hole, leaving the quilt top fuzzy.

WHY USE IT: Bearding is not something you want to occur, so when you see it happening, take time to fix it on the spot.

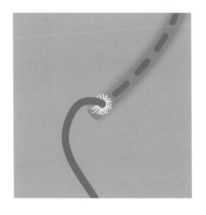

 SEE ALSO: Batting/Wadding, page 123; Quilting, page 88

INDEX

INDEX

ACKNOWLEDGMENTS

This book was made better thanks to every sewing student I have taught over the years. Without all of you, I would be half the teacher and seamstress I am today, and I hope this book serves as a helpful resource for all those questions you ponder along your sewing journey.

I owe a great deal of thanks to the lovely team at RotoVision: Isheeta Mustafi, Tamsin Richardson, and Angela Koo, who keep me on track, edit my words, and serve as a wonderful team to collaborate with.

A tremendous thank you also to Sarah Lawrence and Rob Brandt for the lovely illustrations throughout the book. I adore them, especially all the garment details that get this clothing-loving lady excited about sewing!

And thanks as always to my amazing friends and family for their constant love and support, and to my love Mike, for keeping me going with long champagne-filled days of joy.

ABOUT THE AUTHOR

Christine Haynes is a Los Angeles-based sewing author, teacher, and pattern designer with her own line of sewing patterns—Christine Haynes Patterns—which are perfect for the vintage-loving modern seamstress. She has written three previous books: *Skirts & Dresses for First Time Sewers* (2015, Barron's), *The Complete Photo Guide to Clothing Construction* (2014, CPI), and *Chic & Simple Sewing* (2009, Potter Craft), and has contributed to other books, such as *One Yard Wonders* (2009, Storey). Christine's articles have been published in *Sewstylish*, *Sew News*, *Craftstylish*, and *Craft Zine* magazines, and she is a regular contributor to the Craftsy blog. She teaches sewing classes both in person and online, and has presented lectures and workshops at the American Sewing Guild Conference as well as the 2012–2015 Craftcation Conferences. Christine was a featured guest on seasons 2 and 8 of PBS's *Sew It All* TV show, and her work has been featured in *Threads* magazine, the *New York Times*, the *New York Post*, the *Los Angeles Times*, Martha Stewart's radio network, *People.com*, *LA Weekly*, *Daily Candy*, and NBC's *Today Show*, among others.